SHADOW SOVEREIGNS

To Nick

SHADOW SOVEREIGNS

How Global Corporations Are Seizing Power

Susan George

polity

This book first published in French under the title *Les Usurpateurs: Comment les entreprises transnationales prennent le pouvoir*, Le Seuil, Paris, 2014

First published in English in 2015 by Polity Press

Polity Press
65 Bridge Street
Cambridge CB2 1UR, UK

Polity Press
350 Main Street
Malden, MA 02148, USA

ISBN-13: 978-0-7456-9781-9
ISBN-13: 978-0-7456-9782-6(pb)

A catalogue record for this book is available from the British Library.

Library of Congress Cataloging-in-Publication Data

George, Susan.
Shadow sovereigns : how global corporations are seizing power / Susan George.
pages cm
Includes bibliographical references and index.
ISBN 978-0-7456-9781-9 (hardback : alk. paper) -- ISBN 978-0-7456-9782-6
(pbk. : alk. paper) 1. International business enterprises--Political aspects. 2. Business and politics. 3. International economic relations. 4. Economic policy. 5. Foreign relations. 6. Corporations--Political aspects. I. Title.
HD2755.5.G465 2015
338.8'8--dc23
2014047148

Typeset in 10.75 on 14 pt Gill Sans by
Servis Filmsetting Ltd, Stockport, Cheshire
Printed and bound in the UK by CPI Group (UK) Ltd, Croydon,CR0 4YY

The publisher has used its best endeavours to ensure that the URLs for external websites referred to in this book are correct and active at the time of going to press. However, the publisher has no responsibility for the websites and can make no guarantee that a site will remain live or that the content is or will remain appropriate.

Every effort has been made to trace all copyright holders, but if any have been inadvertently overlooked the publisher will be pleased to include any necessary credits in any subsequent reprint or edition.

For further information on Polity, visit our website:
politybooks.com

CONTENTS

In the course of my life I have developed five little democratic questions. [Ask a powerful person]: 'What power have you got? Where did you get it from? In whose interests do you exercise it? To whom are you accountable? And how can we get rid of you?' If you cannot get rid of the people who govern you, you do not live in a democratic system.

Tony Benn, 1925–2014, Farewell
speech to Parliament, 2001

INTRODUCTION

We're surrounded. Everywhere you look you find masses, droves, gangs of unelected, unaccountable, profit-oriented individuals, corporations and new institutions surfacing everywhere, making official policy in areas ranging from public health to food and agriculture; from taxes to finance and trade. Some are lobbyists for particular private companies or for entire industries, others executives of the world's largest businesses, often with a turnover much greater than the Gross Domestic Product (GDP) of many of the countries where they operate; more and more often, the entities they have created have become quasi-governmental bodies cooperating across national frontiers.

Their role is overtly political and they exercise illegitimate power. They work through lobbies but also directly through governments – not just by convincing elected officials to pass this law or that one, but also through obscure 'expert committees' or ad hoc bodies whose quiet 'mission creep' may gain them official standing. Their activities may be carried out for the benefit of a single company or for an entire industry. Sometimes they form their own powerful international organizations with large budgets devoted to intervention in world affairs. They have become expert in the careful preparation of strategic trade treaties to be negotiated in secret but under the constant surveillance of corporate delegates.

They've got ordinary citizens under their broad thumb, an appendage also used to thumb their noses at the public interest and the common good. Throughout North America and Europe in particular, this corporate spawn is spearheading an important political shift that I call the 'rise of illegitimate authority', and the constellations of organized interest groups constitute a genuine threat to democracy.

I am not against private enterprise. Business is all very well in its proper sphere. But government in the usual sense, carried out by clearly identifiable, democratically elected officials, is gradually being eroded, sometimes even supplanted by shadow 'governments' to which these officials have made huge concessions. This may happen by choice, because officialdom is scared of the giants or admires and wants to pander to them. To be more generous, the bureaucrats and leadership may simply be blind to the long-term implications of their choices. In any case, they have handed over substantial power to these behemoths that now make decisions in innumerable areas that affect our lives.

I've chosen to call these giant corporate actors 'transnationals', or 'TNCs', rather than 'multinationals', which many people use; first, because TNC is the official United Nations usage; more importantly, because the executives who occupy the upper, strategic levels of the largest companies are usually natives of the same country as that of their international headquarters. The companies they run are certainly 'multi'-national in the sense that they have offices, sales and production facilities in a 'multi'-tude of countries, but their top people retain their most relevant family, social, political and cultural connections in the country where they were born and brought up. They understand how to operate there and have easier access and closer relationships with the government. They will lose less time getting things done in the corporate interest.

For such reasons, the CEO, COO, CFO – Chief Executive, Operations or Financial Officers – like the heads of R&D or executive board members, are more likely to be nationals of the headquarters country than to be foreigners, even nearby foreigners. In this sense, even among the largest corporate entities, Nestlé is Swiss, Total French, General Motors American and Siemens German, no matter how many countries they may operate in.

Perhaps locals are also considered potentially more loyal, although to succeed in the business world such virtues as patriotism or loyalty are necessarily reserved for the company itself. Top executives have scant concern for the ultimate fate of any of the countries where the company has facilities, including their own. If higher profits demand it, they must and will readily close down plants or sack workers, whether fellow-citizens or not.

Since the onset of neoliberal politics at the beginning of the 1980s, which accelerated at the end of the Cold War in 1991 when the Soviet Union disappeared, the number of TNCs has soared. Globalization has given wings to the giant corporations and helped them to create their own meta-organizations to deal with particular world spheres such as trade and the environment. Other outgrowths are both 'meta' – above or beyond in Greek – and 'mega' – great or powerful – such as the World Economic Forum (WEF), better known by the name of the Swiss skiing resort where since 1971 it has met yearly: Davos. The growing ambition of the Davos cluster of organizations can be simply defined: to run the world.

I call the WEF habitués the 'Davos Class' because they constitute a genuine social class with the usual attributes expected thereof. The people that make up this class are thus international and nomadic, but they are also a recognizable tribe with their own codes and markers. They have their own languages, not just their native one plus corporatese, but also fluent English. They attended the same or similar universities and business schools, send their children to the same or similar private schools, favour their own watering holes and vacation spots, possess upscale homes in various sophisticated world-class cities, frequent the same meetings (with Davos a must), develop comparable corporate cultures and, of course, have plenty of money.

They are also replaceable – if the man you met in Davos last year is not there this year, then he is no longer President of Bank X or Board Chair of Corporation Y. About 85 per cent of the Davos denizens come from corporations and banks – most of the rest are politicians and there is a smattering of trade unionists, a few acceptable, non-wave-making NGO (nongovernmental organization) people and, for glamour, the occasional movie star.

Unless and until proven wrong, I don't believe in conspiracies, but I definitely believe in *interests* – and that readers are fully capable of distinguishing between the two. A paranoid tale of conspiracy and a factual description of growing corporate power are quite different, even though the latter's signs are all around us and may be difficult to discern for the average person. I hope to provide some clues in these pages. One could write volumes about the TNCs, and the volume of information, alas, grows daily. My goal here is to open the door, not to visit every nook and cranny of the enormous transnational power house.

Before we enter, it's perhaps useful to speak a little about politics in the broadest sense. My chosen subtitle was to have been 'The Rise of Illegitimate Authority', and it's only honest to devote part of this introduction to my motivations and the politics I hope to defend through a factual description of what the TNCs are up to. Like virtually all my work, this book is about power – who has it, how they use it and to what ends. The power of the TNCs is grounded in the spoken or unspoken ideology known as neoliberalism which is itself profoundly anti-democratic. I want to spell this out and will make some brief distinctions between which authority is legitimate and democratic and which isn't. These may seem obvious, but are also often hidden. Readers will already be well aware of the principles involved.

Then I'll explain why I believe that evidence shows illegitimate authority to be on the rise and democracy to be in serious danger of succumbing to the neoliberal disease. This book concerns the United States and Europe because that is where the great majority of corporations are headquartered and because Westerners live where this ideology is most entrenched. We are confronted by a battle between two models of thought and behaviour. Now we have reached the point where we must choose between the Enlightenment heritage developed since the eighteenth century, on the one hand, and, on the other, what I see as the Great Neoliberal Regression. The Enlightenment tradition is losing, and since I've dealt with this subject more thoroughly in earlier work, this description will be short.

The rest of the book will provide concrete examples of how the functions of legitimate government are progressively being taken over by illegitimate, unelected, opaque agents and organizations. Here the list is constantly lengthening. Its treatment cannot be exhaustive, but it will at least try to show that certain patterns and developments are worth watching. The focus will be on power unaccompanied by accountability; power not required to report to anyone excepting its paymasters concerning its activities and which, being difficult to observe and understand, is equally difficult to counteract. If we hope ever to get the dominant corporations under control, we must first be in agreement and sure of the philosophical and ethical underpinnings upon which we base our demands.

WHAT MAKES POWER LEGITIMATE?

In the Enlightenment tradition, legitimacy depends on democracy and the consent of the governed – otherwise, all forms of rule are merely variations on the theme of oppression whether called tyranny, autocracy, dictatorship or what have you. Illegitimate power in the sense I will use it here specifically excludes tyrannies, dictatorships, one-party authoritarian states and so on – we won't deal with overt political power grabs and those who usurp the normal functions of government. This book merely describes some corporate, profit-oriented bodies and their various organizational servants and outgrowths that assume powers formerly reserved for elected officials or state bureaucracies.

The subtlety of illegitimate power and its capacity to act behind the scenes make it hard to give it a single name – although you could call it 'corporatocracy'. It rarely stems from explicit official decisions; its establishment is almost always gradual, barely perceptible and not usually felt as oppression or usurpation by those who submit to it, knowingly or not.

Here are a few quick distinctions between the legitimate and democratic and the illegitimate and undemocratic. Like all writers and most readers, I know that language isn't innocent and ask the reader's indulgence to get two of my pet hatreds out of the way immediately. The first is 'governance'. Government – a perfectly clear word understood by everybody – is increasingly replaced by 'governance', which is an underhand way of changing its meaning.

Governance in old English or old French did have a connotation of statecraft and of keeping public order, but the word mostly designated personal conduct, the governance of a person's behaviour, children, household, etc. The word got adopted by business in the 1970s in the phrase 'corporate governance' and has gained ground ever since. The European Commission –

another unelected body – uses 'governance' almost exclusively as if it were the same thing as government. It isn't. As some wit has put it, 'Governance is the art of governing without government', which is what the Commission does every day. Partly, I think it hopes to avoid such thorny issues as mentioning 'government', which in Europe has implied democracy for a couple of centuries now and which present-day Europe severely lacks. The word is also useful for allowing all manner of extraneous influences and entities to manage the business of running the EU's affairs, corporations chief among them.

My second lexical hatred is for 'stakeholder'. Non-native English speakers are to be excused if they use it: they don't necessarily realize that in English a *stake* is always concerned with money, property or a bet of some kind. In the days of the American frontier, a pioneer moving West could lay, or 'stake', a claim to land – marking it physically with posts, or stakes at the corners. He then held a 'stake'; today, like any stockholder, you can still buy a stake in a company. If you're a gambler at the races, you might tell your neighbour 'I've got a stake in that horse' because you've made a bet on it, or tell a group of friends you don't want to join their poker game because you could lose a lot of money – the stakes are too high.

This word too is a gift for the corporations. Legally, the law (and the profits) of a corporation holds that its fiduciary duty is to increase 'shareholder value'. This distinctive requirement leaves out what the company may do to its workers or to the environment in order to attain that end. As long as they increase shareholder value and are not actually illegal, whatever measures the company chooses to employ are OK. Stakeholders were invented by business to accompany, at least nominally, shareholders. Their stakeholders could be workers, suppliers, customers and so on.

A stakeholder is therefore first someone who holds a proprietary, commercial or financial interest in a private entity. He

or she is surely also a *citizen* somewhere, but the two categories do not necessarily overlap and the term definitely does
not include the general public or the body politic. Again, the
European Commission uses 'stakeholder' constantly, trying to
make it synonymous with 'citizen'. As the Commission doubtless realizes and tries to hide, a citizen is someone who has not
only a material *interest* but also a political, civic and moral *right*
to participate in the government and the affairs of their town,
country or region.

If you want proof, just try being a stakeholder – in, say, the
treaty negotiations between the European Union (EU) and the
United States, which we'll look at more closely later on. You
won't even be allowed a glance at the documents, much less
a seat at the table or a channel to express your own views.
Citizens are born that way; stakeholders are only stakeholders
if the real power-holders say they are.

Here, now, is a quick 'legitimacy' checklist that virtually all
Westerners – and a great many others – would accept. The
hallmarks of legitimate power are: free and fair elections for
designating officials to represent the people, constitutional government, the rule of law, equality before the law; separation of
executive, legislative and judicial powers, checks and balances to
prevent any one part of government from becoming too powerful, the separation of church and state. All these are crowned by
the general notion of the 'consent of the governed'. People are
supposed to have the right to change their government if they
don't like the one they have, through elections, petitions, dem-
onstrations and so on. If they are very lucky, their constitution
will also contain provisions for referenda, citizen initiative and
other participatory mechanisms.

Coupled with such provisions is the never-completed, always
expanding list of individual and collective rights and freedoms as
first set out in the French Declaration of the Rights of Man and
of the Citizen of 1789 and the Bill of Rights of 1791 compris-

ing the first 10 amendments to the Constitution of the United States of America. These make explicit and legally secure such ideas as freedom of opinion, speech, worship, the press and so on. All these ideas were once considered revolutionary, as indeed they were, even when still woefully incomplete. At the time of the Declaration in France and the Bill of Rights in America, slavery still existed, women and minorities could not vote or exercise most rights, censorship was rampant and so on. But the notions of individual rights and freely elected governments that are obliged to protect and guarantee them are a vital part of the movement of the Enlightenment and an equally vital pillar of legitimate authority.

Depending on how far back one wants to go, the first stirrings of this movement can be dated from the seventeenth century or even earlier, but most see the Enlightenment as an eighteenth-century achievement. Its central thinkers defended the notion not just of rights and freedoms, but also of duties and norms of conduct for individual citizens and that of the common good. From these derive the famous French motto of *Liberté* (so long as you don't infringe on the *Liberté* of others), *Egalité* (where the law is concerned – don't expect it in the distribution of property) and *Fraternité* (or solidarity), especially with those less fortunate because we all are part of a common body and a common endeavour. These thinkers also defended rational thought and the scientific method against dogma and superstition and invented totally new concepts such as collective progress and individual happiness – radically new concepts at the time.[1]

WHY DEFEND THIS MODEL?

I believe we must preserve and improve the democratic, Enlightenment model and believe further that it is gravely threatened by illegitimate power. After the end of the Great

Depression and of World War II, it seemed that the battles of the previous century and a half to extend democracy and expand our rights would never need to be fought again. Somehow the ghosts of the French revolutionaries and members of the National Council of the Resistance, of Franklin Roosevelt's New Dealers and John Maynard Keynes were watching over us. The welfare state wasn't perfect, but it was still by far the best thing the West had ever seen. Decolonization was progressing and the idea of 'development' for the poorer countries gave hope for the future. That view turned out to be naive. Little by little over the past few decades a new set of values has gradually taken centre stage, along with a great many changes for the worse in government.

Now standing against the Enlightenment model is *a new ideology of selfishness, greed and cruelty* – the Great Neoliberal Regression. It has steadily gained ground despite overwhelming proof that it is harmful to nearly everyone, except for the extremely wealthy, the topmost people on the corporate ladder and those who enrich themselves by manipulating money in the international casino economy. I did not foresee that such people, or such a system, could emerge not just unscathed but even stronger after the financial tsunami which struck in 2007–8 and with whose dismal aftermaths we still live. But this is what has happened.[2]

The neoliberal model makes false promises of prosperity and jobs for all but is both unable and unwilling to deliver. It has been thoroughly discredited – discredited intellectually, empirically and morally. Its theoretical and scientific or economic basis is nonexistent – even the International Monetary Fund (IMF) has published several papers to that effect – its practical consequences are harmful to the great majority and its morality indefensible if one still believes that the goal of government should be to strive for a fair society providing the greatest possible good for the greatest possible number.

Despite its manifest failures, the Great Neoliberal Regression has triumphed and continues to cause huge shifts of wealth and power in favour of the already richest and most powerful individuals, classes and corporations, while wreaking havoc for the middle class and the unprotected. One of the most recent findings in this direction is that of the gains from growth that have occurred since the crisis of 2007–8 in the USA: 95 per cent has gone to the top 1 per cent of Americans.[3]

In all the OECD countries, but particularly in the United States and Great Britain, inequalities have increased. In Europe, the shares of economic value produced in a given year and distributed between capital and labour have shifted drastically. In the 1970s, the share of value going to labour in the form of wages and salaries in Europe was about 70 per cent of the annual European GDP. The remaining 30 per cent went to capital in the form of dividends, profits and rents. Today, capital receives at least 40 per cent of GDP – in some countries more – and labour gets 60 per cent or less.

These 10 per cent gains for capital and losses for labour are not small change. Since the yearly economic product of Europe is about €13 trillion, ten points less of GDP means that European salaried people are losing about €1.3 trillion in revenues every year compared to what they would have received without such changes. The difference goes to capital. Corporate shareholders used to be content with dividends representing a return of 3 or 4 per cent a year; now the largest of them demand 10–12 per cent and more. The former goal of building a strong, healthy and lasting business enterprise well integrated into the community has been replaced by the single imperative of 'shareholder value', which encourages short-termism, asset stripping, mass layoffs and other negative consequences.

Furthermore, if working people had continued to receive those 10 points of GDP, our economies would be totally transformed. If the distribution of economic value were the same as in the 1970s, an extra €1,300 billion would have poured into the real economy every year simply because wages and salaries go overwhelmingly into the purchase of goods and services or longer-term purchases such as houses. This spending is what keeps our economies ticking over. We could have financed public investments in services underpinning the common good and the infrastructure to create a green transition to a low or zero-carbon economy.

Today, at the urging of neoliberal regression enthusiasts, politicians actually *favour* policies guaranteed to lead to high unemployment and social breakdown. The wages of those who do have work are stagnant and sometimes falling, particularly in Southern Europe but even for a sizeable part of the German working class. Youth unemployment has reached dramatic levels. The wages of working people cannot possibly keep irrigating the economy, except for necessities. Capital on the other hand is reinvested, frequently in the purchase of financial products which create no social value, have little or nothing to do with the real economy and, as we have all too recently seen, can bring that real economy to its knees.

The next time someone proclaims that 'labour is too expensive', ask them why nobody ever says the same about capital – that is where the wealth has gone and it has never demanded such high remuneration.

Transnational corporations represent neoliberal practice in its purest form, and this is why I believe they must be got under control. I don't say downsized or destroyed, but at least prevented from taking over the business of government. TNCs want deregulation and freedom from government oversight to the greatest possible extent and are writing the legal instruments to obtain it. They want the weakest possible labour unions or, where feasible, none at all. They want to take over public services and claim that their privatization is desirable because private enterprise can always be counted on to outperform public services on criteria of efficiency, quality, availability and price.

Corporate doctrine holds that free trade may have temporary drawbacks for some but will ultimately serve the entire population well through growth, more and better jobs and greater wealth. Both tariff and nontariff barriers to trade and to foreign direct investment should be removed; investors should be granted the right to sue any government if its policies restrict profits. Products and services traded today are overregulated and these measures, which the Americans call 'trade irritants', must be reduced to a minimum and 'harmonized', towards the lowest common denominator.

Companies often receive government subsidies but are against spending on social services (although not on defence and national security). The public sector in general should be reduced. Government debt and government budget deficits have accumulated because 'we have been living beyond our means' – not because we have had to pay for a colossal financial crisis and its consequences – of their making.

They don't care much for taxes either. In the USA, Ronald Reagan famously initiated the principle that 'government is the problem, not the solution'. Today, this is an article of faith among those whom James Surowiecki, a staff writer for the *New Yorker*, has named the 'moaning moguls'. One of them compared taxation to 'the German invasion of Poland'. They also make plain their resentment of criticism from the middle class or upstarts such as the Occupy movement; two of them likening such criticism to 'the Nazis' attacks on the Jews'.[4]

Austerity programmes are based on these beliefs, every one of which is factually wrong though endlessly repeated. Aside from the fact that it doesn't work and cannot create a healthy economy serving everyone, neoliberalism is selfish and cruel, even antihuman. It is the reason why Greek pensioners today are searching rubbish bins for food by mid-month because they can no longer afford to buy it. In the USA, a Tennessee Republican voted to eliminate food stamps, using words like those of some harsh biblical prophet: 'Those who refuse to work shall not eat.' He said nothing about the lack of jobs available for those trying to find work.

In the EU, a fully developed offensive against the welfare state and the European social model is under way, with the goal of clawing back all the gains won by working people over the past six or seven decades. For neoliberals, every aspect of this social model is abhorrent because it consists in taxing the rich and the corporations – those who supposedly have created all the wealth – and giving that wealth to people – or to institutions serving them – who do not deserve it. The poor – even the working poor – are not partners in creating value, but spongers. The rich owe them nothing.

Just as work creates no value, so the Davos class largely considers that their wealth owes nothing to nature. In the neoliberal canon, capital alone, unlike labour and nature, creates value and, therefore, jobs. Both workers and nature exist for the benefit and use of corporate entities. Only investors (i.e., 'shareholders') and the people in top management are value creators. That is why they are also the major stakeholders in any given policy or decision.

How can all this be? How can policies be shown both intellectually and practically not to work yet still continue to reign? Does a policy that 'works' still mean improving the lot of the people and their environment through jobs, social protection, public services and so on? Or need it work only for the elites and the TNCs? Small businesses that provide nearly all the employment don't share in the bonanza. Are we faced here with a kind of religion? The neoliberals can also be seen as theoliberals, as in 'theology'.

Undeniable scientific proof does not and never will exist for any religion. You're a believer or you aren't; you can try to justify your belief, but you can't demonstrate it rigorously. The theo-liberals go one better than religion: all the numbers and the statistics show that people are worse off because of their policies, and yet, through careful and clever packaging, they continue to disseminate their ideas successfully despite these overwhelmingly negative results.[5]

You can extend the religious metaphor as far as you like. For instance, the high priests of this religion can be found in Brussels and Washington, its itinerant missionaries in Davos, its theologians and sermon writers in right-wing think-tanks, its facilitators in innumerable ministries (government, not religious ministries), its practitioners in corporate board-rooms . . . etc.

None of this is to say that democracy is already perfect, much less that Enlightenment values have been respected and upheld. I hope that in the West we shall never forget the dark side of our history. Both 'democracy' and 'Enlightenment values' are used here to represent 'ideal types'. The same Western world during the same period of the flowering of noble ideals also committed unspeakable horrors, starting with the Reign of Terror (La Terreur) of 1793–4. The West was certainly not alone in practising slavery, but it was deeply rooted. Nor did Westerners invent genocide – others have often killed whomsoever they could, and religious wars took their toll – but previous eras lacked our superior technology and the systematic administration of catastrophes such as the Shoah.

We harboured fascist governments and carried out the two bloodiest wars in human history. We colonized most of the known world and cared little for our own poor and excluded who had only their labour power to sell in brutal new industrial economies. Our misconceived remedies for social problems included the deportation of petty criminals and debtors to Australia or the forced outmigration of the impoverished to the New World – even though these may have turned out to be good ideas in the much longer term. With the possible exception of legal slavery, all these evils still threaten us today.[6]

Democracy always has been and always will be a work in progress. Truly equal rights are not yet fully achieved for huge swathes of humanity. Despite all this, democracy based on Enlightenment values still seems to me, and to millions of others, the best and most admirable form of government ever attempted. One proof of this is that other, not necessarily Western, people want the same sort of rules and values-based government for themselves and have shown themselves willing to fight and die to achieve it. Human emancipation is an ongoing story and this model is worth preserving and improving everywhere, including the places where it began. These are precisely the places where new threats to democracy are arising thick and fast and they are the ones which we shall try to introduce now.

WHAT IS REQUIRED FOR AUTHORITY TO BE LEGITIMATE?

At least in Western countries citizens tend to believe – or at least cling to the hope – that they are still living under a democratic system, although the drop in voter participation and the tendency to complain that 'all politicians are the same, dishonest and useless' signifies that many have given up on democracy altogether. Offhand, I would say that maybe 10 per cent of plumbers or professors aren't that good either and there's nothing special about politicians. Most of them are probably trying to do their best, but they are, for sure, giving in more and more to illegitimate authority, wittingly or not.

What does this illegitimate authority want? First, and perhaps paradoxically, as embodied by TNCs, it wants to establish a new brand of legitimacy for the alternative system it is putting in place. Second, it seeks to use that pseudo-legitimacy in order to demolish public services, the public interest and the common good in favour of higher corporate gains and rules better suited to corporate purposes for cornering unlimited wealth and banishing nearly all forms of common, citizen property, including citizen protection.

A broad spectrum of shadowy non-elected people is entrenching neoliberal values and doctrine, orienting government decisions and standing against democracy. In the following pages we'll start with the best known and most traditional – the ordinary lobbies, familiar actors on the fringes of government for a couple of centuries. Then we'll move on to the megalobbies primed to defend sectoral interests through less easily recognized 'foundations' or 'councils', themselves supposedly non-profit but serving overall corporate aims.

Some semi-official bodies are run to favour corporate interests. Take, for example, the International Accounting Standards Board (IASB), surely unknown to practically every European citizen even though its rules influence the taxes a government can collect. The IASB became official through the efforts of a single, ultraliberal, unelected EU commissioner.

Perhaps the most aggressive and dangerous corporate behaviour at present is the takeover of government functions and removal of basic citizen protections through so-called free trade treaties. In July 2013, negotiations began on the Transatlantic Trade and Investment Partnership (TTIP). If ratified, this agreement will make most of the rules that govern some 40 per cent of the world's GDP – the USA plus Europe – and has been in preparation since 1995 under the leadership of the most important TNCs from both sides of the ocean. The investment chapters will grant unprecedented powers to TNCs to bring legal charges against governments in private arbitration tribunals if the corporation believes its present or future profits are threatened by a government decision. We'll also see how the European executive is cooperating with the TNCs to eliminate any regulations European business might want to get rid of.

TNCs today work at the national, regional or European and supranational echelons including that of the United Nations. For decades they have sent large delegations to official UN conferences, but more recently they have built up their own organizations, which are now officially within the UN system. Their penetration of the UN was not sneaky or sly – they were invited in through the front door by the then Secretary-General himself. The instrument is called the United Nations Global Compact (UNGC) and it exemplifies the ambitions of the Davos Class to manage the world.

The WEF is also developing a plan that deals with everything that it sees as ill-managed by governments or intergovernmental bodies – from finance to the law of the sea. TNCs appear to believe that, in many areas, governments should be replaced by far more competent 'multi-stakeholder bodies' that include an important role for business. The self-selected body to manage such a replacement is the Davos class itself, and the WEF's aggressively titled programme is called the Global Redesign Initiative no less – a triumph of modesty and self-effacement.

It's not just their size, their enormous wealth and their assets that make the TNCs dangerous to democracy. It's also their concentration and cohesion, their cooperation and capacity to influence, infiltrate and in some areas virtually replace governments. They are acting as a genuine, international authority in order to defend their commercial interests, power and profits against the common good. They share a common language, a common ideology and common ambitions that affect us all. Citizens who value democracy ignore them at their peril.

I

LOBBIES, MEGA-LOBBIES AND
HOW TO JOIN THEM

Lobbyists are common as houseflies in Washington DC and Brussels. Theirs is not perhaps the world's oldest profession, but they have been around for longer than any of the rest of us and, according to parliamentary lore, started hanging out in the lobby of the House of Commons in the early nineteenth century. In Washington it was a less dignified venue, but still a lobby – that of the Willard Hotel where President Ulysses S. Grant (from 1869 to 1877) liked to go to drink brandy and smoke cigars with his buddies and often with people who wanted something.

HOW IT WORKS IN WASHINGTON

They've improved their techniques, make good money and there's no denying they get results. Today, Washington lobbyists must declare themselves to the Clerk of Congress and register how much they're paid and by whom. The United States first tried to get lobbying under control after the end of

World War II with the Legislative Reorganization Act of 1946, but when officials at the General Accounting Office evaluated the results several years down the road, they found that about 90 per cent of all the lobbyists were paying no attention to its requirements. Eventually, President Bill Clinton signed the Lobbying Disclosure Act of 1995, a bill with real teeth requiring quarterly reports and listings of all contacts with government officials and members of Congress.

In 2008, the Obama administration sought to tighten the law still further. This may have been too much of a good thing. The number of lobbyists listed in the congressional registry has declined from a peak of 14,837 in 2007 to a low point for the decade of 12,341 in 2013. The drop does not seem to be due to cutbacks in lobbying activities – it has occurred because people who are still lobbyists are not registering. The new law left the definition of a 'lobbyist' open to interpretation, and law firms admit they've been helping many clients to deregister. The director of government affairs for the American Bar Association explains that in the pre-Obama legal context, 'people in Washington would have said, "*If in doubt, register . . . [in those days they would think] I like the publicity . . . I want to be able to tell potential clients how many [other clients] I am already registered for.*"' Not any more: One recently deregistered professional says, '*Lobbying isn't a crime. It's a profession and in my view it is an honourable one*', but, he feels, the Obama administration doesn't see it that way. Today, lobbyists who can show they aren't spending more than 20 per cent of their time in direct contact with lawmakers – even though they might be dispatching busloads of employees to do that job – are, according to the *New York Times*, the ones who are no longer registering.[1]

However, and for whatever reason, American lobbying firms are also beginning to hurt financially. In 2009 and 2010 their industry had a stunning turnover of $3.5 billion but by 2013 had lost around $250 million of that bounty. In May 2014, the lobbying blog 'Open Secrets' announced that the first quarter was the 'worst in the last four years, continuing the downward slide of K Street'.[2]

Even so, K Street seems to have little enough to worry about. If I had been asked to guess which industries spent the most on lobbying, I would doubtless have said defence, oil and finance, probably in that order. Dead wrong. Health is, by a long way, the frontrunner, with pharmaceuticals and health products coming in at number one in 2013, at $65.4 million. But if you add to that the separately listed sums spent on lobbying by the categories 'hospitals and nursing homes', 'health professionals and health services' and HMOs (Health Maintenance Organizations), the bill comes to nearly $129 million.[3] And we wonder why the US healthcare system is the most expensive in the world; why so many people are not cared for at all and so many others have become convinced that 'Obamacare' is an infringement of their liberty. It's because lobbyists are good at their jobs and their high-class, invisible brainwashing campaigns work – they work to protect the super-profits of private healthcare providers and insurance companies, and the expenditures end up in the prices of the services or the drugs. For decades now, 'socialized medicine' has been the bogeyman mantra that shuts people up and makes them afraid to support a politician who has the courage to propose public healthcare spending of the kind that obtains in every other civilized and moderately wealthy country in the world.

As for my spontaneous (and wrong) choices of defence, oil and finance as the biggest spenders, defence and aerospace rate only $15.5 million, but the whole complex comes to $30 million. Oil and gas by themselves weigh in at 'only' $34 million, but combined with all 'energy and natural resources' come to $91.4 million. The financial industry is doing better than both defence and oil if all financial sectors such as securities and investment, commercial banks and real estate are added together ($119 million). So my choices were mistaken, but that could also be at least partly because the big firms in these sectors know they'll get what they want, lobbying or no lobbying.

IT COST US $5 BILLION BUT WE WON: LOBBYING TO CREATE A REALLY SPECTACULAR FINANCIAL CRISIS

However much the banks and funds may actually be spending on lobbying today, they have a proven capacity for endangering the rest of us and a long history of doing so. From the mid-1980s onwards, no doubt emboldened by the rising tide of neoliberalism, the largest American banking, securities, insurance and accounting TNCs joined forces, employed nearly 3,000 people and spent roughly $5 billion to get rid of a dozen New Deal laws passed in the 1930s under the Roosevelt administration. These laws were precisely those that had protected the American economy from catastrophe for more than 60 years.

That shield was shattered thanks to their collective lobbying push. Incredibly, the financial corporations won the freedom to remove money-losing assets from their balance-sheets and place them in 'shadow' or undeclared banks, where even their shareholders would never find them. They could create and trade, with no regulation whatsoever, hundreds of billions of dollars worth of toxic 'derivative' products, based on huge piles of consumer debts such as bundles of sub-prime mortgages.

For near-total financial ruin, one can't surpass the fall of the Glass-Steagall Act of 1933, without a doubt the financial lobbying coup of the twentieth century. This New Deal measure had separated commercial (retail) banks from investment banks, and it remained in place until President Clinton signed the act that abrogated it in 1999. The financial lobby had pushed to obtain this for a dozen years before Clinton finally complied. He was vigorously backed, or shoved, by Federal Reserve chairman Alan

Greenspan, not to mention his chief economic advisor Larry Summers and, above all, his treasury secretary Robert Rubin, formerly chairman of Goldman Sachs.[4]

The coup soon enough fell on the backs of governments and their taxpayers. Mega-takeovers, mergers and acquisitions immediately followed the end of Glass-Steagall, creating gigantic structures which thus became 'too big to fail', according to the now-classic phrase. The banks didn't even call themselves 'banks' anymore, but 'financial services corporations', and they knew they could concentrate henceforward on creating the casino economy unsupervised and unrestrained. They had just added countless pots of gold to their hoards and could speculate with their customers' deposits. All the newly legal mergers gave predator capitalists the right to play with everybody's money.

They knew, first, that if their bets went wrong, the government would have to jump in and save them; second, that they were ideally placed: too big to fail, but not too big to bail. It turned out later that they were also too powerful to jail – some banks paid fines, but no bankers went to jail for their part in creating the crisis.

Such are the victories lobbying can achieve. It reminds one of the high official who castigated, 'business and financial monopoly, speculation, reckless banking . . . [these businesses] had begun to consider the government of the United States as a mere appendage to their own affairs.' That was Franklin Roosevelt in 1936.[5]

The financial crash had a severe impact on countries far distant from the USA, particularly in Europe, but for sheer mass mayhem, the lobbyists hadn't finished. Nearly anything could now become a 'derivative'.[6] Futures trading of such commodities as wheat, corn and soya had for decades, not to say centuries, tended to the usefully boring – and their 'volatility' was measured in pennies per day. But as soon as certain factors pointed to reduced food supplies, rampant speculation invaded the commodities markets. Thanks to the work of the financial lobby brigades, traders and speculators could purchase unlimited futures contracts on foodstuffs.

Previously, rules and compulsory declarations had prevented anyone from 'cornering the market' and manipulating prices. But lobbyists got rid of all that nonsense. Congress passed the Commodities Futures Modernization Act in December 2000 when President Clinton was leaving the White House and George W. Bush was waiting on the threshold. 'Modernization' can be freely translated as 'total deregulation': the new legislation replaced three venerable New Deal laws that had kept commodities markets relatively stable since the 1930s.

Consequently, in 2008, when several factors pointed towards reduced food production, Wall Street moved fast and poured money into the commodities market. In March 2003, a relatively modest $13 billion had been riding on foodstuffs; five years later, in March 2008, the figure was $260 billion – 20 times as much. During the single day of 27 March, the price of wheat skyrocketed by a remarkable 31 per cent.

Experts estimated that, depending on the commodity, Wall Street controlled 20–50 per cent of all the foodstuffs traded. Sudden price surges may not be too big a deal in developed countries, where food accounts for just 10–15 per cent of the cost of living – but in import-dependent places, where most of the population spends closer to 70 or 80 per cent on food, they are a national disaster. According to the UN Food and Agriculture Organization (FAO), the doubling or tripling of the cost of food staples pushed another 100 million people across the fine line between survival and chronic hunger. Food riots occurred in more than 30 very different countries throughout the world.

DEMOCRACY AT A STANDSTILL: NIMTOO RULES

Roosevelt's words about financial monopolies seeing the US government as 'a mere appendage to their own affairs' accurately describe our present situation. Since the fall of Lehman Brothers, virtually nothing has been done to reregulate finance. Meanwhile, derivatives trading has reached $2,300,000,000,000 *per day*, a daily turnover 30 per cent higher than in 2007 when the crisis began. These financial products are recognized as the major culprits in nearly bringing down the world's entire banking system and their market turnover (or 'notional value') has reached an unimaginable $700 trillion per year. How much is that? The GDP of the entire world is estimated at about $70 trillion, so the circulation of this single class of financial products is 10 times greater.

Currency trading is also up by a third since the year the crisis broke, at well over five trillion dollars a day.[7] A lot of these trades are automated, micro-second, algorithm-triggered deals that can create other hazards because even robots make mistakes. These figures are not from progressive or scaremongering sources, but from the Triennial Surveys of the staid and sober Bank for International Settlements, the latest published in early 2014. Finance has gone far beyond acceptable limits; it is less (and less well) regulated than any other industry; it may easily lead us to another catastrophe that would make 2007–8 look like a minor hiccup.

Everybody who could do something about the situation knows all this; their action is nonetheless limited to keeping their fingers crossed and clinging to the NIMTOO hope: Not In My Term Of Office. This is one conclusive proof of the triumph of lobbies that can now regulate governments rather than being regulated by them.[8]

Clearly we are asking for trouble and there is now mathematical proof of this scary prospect. Complex systems researchers at the Zurich Polytechnic have mapped 'The Network of Global Corporate Control' and discovered that the most powerful and interconnected corporations in the world are almost all financial.[9] Without going into detail, let me first reassure you that you can, if you wish, read their paper and skip the equations as I did; you can also cut to the Annex for the list of the 50 most interconnected corporations worldwide. These painstaking researchers started with the Orbis database of 37 million companies, prised out the 43,000 TNCs, traced their interlocking ownership, reduced their list to 1,318 companies, each connected to an average of 20 others; they reduced these still further to 147 'super-entities' that controlled 40 per cent of the total wealth in the entire network. The top 50 of the supers are the quintessentially linked corporations; they embody what the authors term the 'knife-edge property'. If all is well in the economy, the total structure looks robust, but if a shock strikes one of them, the shockwaves will immediately propagate and the earthquake will be unleashed. Chilling detail: Lehman Brothers is on the list because the mathematicians were using a database dating from 2007, showing that, yes, you can fall off the knife-edge and land on the wrong side. This isn't sci-fi or conspiracy theory. This is science and it's shouting at us to get the financial lobby under control.[10]

A VISIT TO BACKWARD EUROPE

The USA may be the lobbying playground of the world, it may be governed by its banks, but in terms of regulating lobbies – or at least individual lobbyists – Washington is the clear winner and Brussels is a half-century behind. With no register at all for most of its existence, the EU in 2008 introduced a 'voluntary' register, which is laughable – and risky for the public as well.

By mid-2013, according to an EU parliamentary library source, nearly 5,700 lobbying organizations had registered.

They belong to various categories classed as consultancies and law firms, 'in-house' lobbyists and trade or professional associations, think-tanks and research institutes, NGOs, public organizations representing local, regional, municipal or mixed interests, and, finally, religious organizations.[11] All are expected to endorse a code of conduct when they sign up and can be automatically disbarred if they do not provide yearly updates. The Joint Transparency Register Secretariat can receive complaints and alerts and runs random 'quality checks' which have so far led to about 100 organizations being disbarred.

Such measures, in the view of ALTER-EU, a coalition of NGOs campaigning for transparency in EU policymaking, may be a start, but they are still sadly deficient. The NGO members have identified a lot of well-known Brussels lobbyists not on the list, incomplete and inaccurate information and a code of conduct full of loopholes.

A German MEP was named in 2012 to head a parliamentary working group for reviewing the voluntary register. He eventually alerted the parliament's president Martin Schulz to the fact that the major obstacle standing in the way of a compulsory register was easily identified: it was being 'inhibited by the Commission' itself. This letter to Schulz was leaked: the working group wanted the parliament to tell the Commission it should 'promote a political action aimed at the creation of a new legal basis . . . for a mandatory lobbying register'. Why such a convoluted approach? They apparently had no choice. The Commission's legal services had pre-empted them by handing down the opinion that the EU's treaties do not allow for a compulsory register. This legal judgment – in which the legal services of the parliament also joined – was the excuse to prevent a register from even being proposed.[12]

The EU's treaties, as anyone who has ever timidly opened them knows, are so long, so complex and so intricate they can provide a legal basis for just about anything except possibly murdering a commissioner. The Commission doesn't want a compulsory register that would release details about who lobbies whom because such details would implicate the Commission itself, period.

The illegality argument is a delaying ploy and, as the MEP told Schulz, 'in the light of a difficult situation', the parliament should take a strong stand and tell the Commission that it wanted a new legal basis for a compulsory register and set a timeline. The new rules ought to be in place by the first of January 2015 and 'in case the Commission fails to reach this goal' (as seems more than likely), it should be told to submit a proposal for a compulsory register on a new legal basis 'by the end of 2016'. As of June 2014, a new parliament was in place, a different working group on a mandatory lobbying register must be named and the merry-go-round can start spinning again.[13]

Informal estimates say that 10–15,000 lobbyists are talking non-stop to EU parliamentarians, commissioners and various civil servants in the directorates. They push for junk food, genetically manipulated crops, tobacco, dangerous chemicals or dicey pharmaceuticals, the biggest greenhouse gas emitters, the biggest banks and whatever else European TNCs are desirous of obtaining. Some 'good-guy' non-profits also maintain lobbyists to defend the environment, human or consumer rights, labour standards and other worthy endeavours, but they are a small minority.

The point is that we still have no direct knowledge of the real number of lobbyists in Europe, much less what they spend or who they talk to. And large organizations like BusinessEurope, even if they register, will register only once, declare however many euros they choose and never have to admit that they will be constantly deploying people to virtually all the directorates to move whatever agendas they find relevant.

HOW DO THEY DO IT?

Lobbying is an industry; it is also a science, an art and clients hire lobbyists because they know they have mastered a host of techniques and skills. The following remarks may sound like truisms to seasoned observers, but provide a handy guide for anyone who seeks to penetrate this shadowy world and expose it to the daylight. Start from the principle that the less the public notices lobbyists and their activities, the more successful they are in serving the interests of their paymasters. What follows are a few lobbying commandments.

Above all, remember that your mission is to write new legislation or hold up any move by regulators or reformers that might harm the interests of your paymasters. Delay is often the best tactic and even avoiding new legislation or preserving the status quo should satisfy your clients.

Seize control of the debate from the outset and frame it so that you can win the arguments. Your own vocabulary should set the terms and the limits of discussion. Provide no space for arguments you can't win. Base your claims on semi-facts or outright lies if you have to. Whoever checks won't have the same access to decision-makers you have. If, for example, a product or process is anti-environmental to the core, don't refer to the environment – talk about jobs and growth. In fact, talk about jobs and growth no matter what the subject. If you are pushing, for example, for the privatization of a public service, stress that private will be better than public in terms of quality, access, reliability and cost. Nine chances out of ten this is a lie, but one that cannot be proven until too late.

Always remember that you are not speaking for a special interest or – heaven forbid – the 1 per cent. Use class arguments judiciously – never let it be said or even thought that the principle beneficiary of your proposal will actually be a tiny, well-identified minority, a specific sector, an individual company. You are at all times defending the common good, the national interest and ordinary people, otherwise known as 'consumers' or 'taxpayers'; sometimes 'sufferers' or even 'victims'. Consumers are kings/queens and must never be deprived of their 'freedom of choice' – for example, to eat rubbish food and smoke or drink themselves to death. Furthermore, if the other side – the one opposed to your solution – wins this argument, their proposal will cost far more than yours. Taxpayers – all of us poor working people – will foot the bill.

If we don't do it – plant genetically manipulated organisms (GMOs), frack, etc. – neighbouring countries will. Our compet-i-tiv-i-ty will suffer and this is the principle economic virtue for which any government should strive because it is the way to create jobs and growth. If, on the contrary, we do it, preferably before the others, it will benefit absolutely everyone.

If you are campaigning for tobacco, alcohol, chemicals, greenhouse gas emitters and the like, you must learn to *distort the science*. Generally, the scientific facts have been all too well established and you will be working against heavy odds. Remember, however, that creating doubt in the public's mind about even the best-established scientific facts is usually all it takes: you do not have to convince everyone and you do not need to establish certainty, just uncertainty. If the evidence is incontrovertible, as it eventually became in the case of smoking, accept it and work around it.

However, most of the time, *everything* in science – with the possible exception of the $2 + 2 = 4$ variety – can be exposed to uncertainty because that is the very nature of the scientific method. If you aren't a sceptic, you aren't a scientist, because science without the permanent stance of doubt would be more like religion. Even a result that seemed utterly and firmly substantiated can be called back into question by new evidence, as happened in 2013–14, for example, in the case of the Big Bang.

From your point of view as a lobbyist, this is a good thing. It is what allows Creationists to claim that evolution according to Darwin is 'just a hypothesis', which is true. It's a hypothesis that has mountains of evidence in its favour, whereas there is none at all for Creationism (or its more subtle variety 'intelligent design'), but many people do not understand this distinction. Darwin himself is said to have been so astounded by the extraordinary complexity and design of the human eye that he felt it might call his theory of evolution into doubt. The 'just a hypothesis' argument has already shown itself to be devastating in the case, for example, of climate change – about which more in a moment.

As a lobbyist, you can use other tricks where science is concerned. You can hire tame or venal scientists to write articles that support your clients' theses. If necessary, you can sometimes get them published in mainstream media by bullying and accusing them of 'not presenting their readers or viewers with all sides of the question' or using arguments of 'minority rights' even if the minority is one in ten thousand. Peer-reviewed, genuine scientific journals can be harder to crack, but there have been cases where editors are beholden to certain commercial concerns. Tame scientists can also initiate and circulate petitions or write letters to the editor of the mainstream or scientific press.

Exercise caution nonetheless. It could be dangerous for you, the lobbyist, to use scientists employed by your own employer.

George Monbiot in his column for the *Guardian* once revealed that Monsanto's lobbyists had used Monsanto's own scientists this way, getting them to sign various documents including letters mentioning their qualifications (PhD, etc.) but not their affiliation. Then again, such tactics will not necessarily come out and, even if exposed, how many people will see the proof?

The good lobbyist knows how to organize 'astro-turf' movements. Astro-turf is fake grass that can be rolled out for football games in sports stadiums and it is to real grass what these artificial movements are to the genuine grass-roots movements created and sustained by real citizens. All kinds of movements have been cobbled together by lobbies, often called 'Americans for This or That'.

If the goal is to defend a product that groups opposed to yours want abolished or at least restricted because it's dangerous or unhealthy, your job is to complain that the consumer's 'freedom to choose' is being infringed by the 'nanny state' that wants to make people's decisions for them. If your goal is to maintain an existing policy or promote a new one, then launch petitions and collect signatures. If, on closer examination, the signatures turn out to be those of corporate employees whose jobs depend on agreeing, should you still take the risk? Yes: who's going to find out? As with the tame scientist, you should recruit the tame sociologist or opinion-maker with impressive credentials to support your proposal.

It may also be helpful to use scaremongering as in 'this legislation will increase costs for business and lead to higher prices and/or unemployment'. This proposal will undermine the family/be harmful to our children, *ad libitum*. The whole campaign must be framed in terms of legitimate 'news' rather than the propaganda operation it is. Consumers and real citizens usually don't take the time to find out who funds a campaign, especially when it can be made to sound benign and legitimate or simply an expression of the constitutional right to freedom of speech.

I witnessed lobbying techniques at work myself in June 2014 at the University of Pretoria in South Africa, where Vandana Shiva, the well-known environmentalist, anti-GMO writer and activist, was speaking. The lobby people had come early and positioned themselves strategically around the lecture theatre (some of the organizers had heard them discussing their game plan together). Quick off the mark when question time came, they tried one after the other from their different places in the hall to discredit Shiva's claims, but also to position the debate where they wanted it to stay. She quickly shut them up with facts and figures, plus some help from the increasingly hostile audience.

After her talk, she told some of us the story of how, visiting the lavatory before a different talk, she had heard a young woman address another – whom Shiva recognized as a pro-GMO lobbyist – as 'Mummy'. At question time, the daughter stood up and explained how her mother was a poor farmer whose harvests were meagre and unreliable and who couldn't pay her school fees. She had, she said, had to leave school because they were so hard up. It was a real tear-jerker. Then, the girl continued, her mother switched to GMO seeds and thanks to them had earned much more on her abundant crops. 'Would you rather my mother was still poor and I couldn't go to school?' she asked Shiva. Vandana calmly replied that she was not a poor woman farmer's daughter at all but the daughter of Ms X the lobbyist who, she announced, pointing a finger, was sitting right *there*. Whereupon the mother cried out 'that's not fair' and the audience dissolved in laughter.

Some tactics I wouldn't have thought of are noted by Tamasin Cave and Andy Rowell in their book *A Quiet Word*, a book about lobbying in Britain, as well as in a piece in the *Guardian*.[14] They report that there is a perception that 'decisions taken in government could be influenced by the reward of future employment'. Top-ranking people in some British government departments are using the revolving door more and more frequently. Department of Health personnel, in particular, are said to be jostling each other to get into the private sector. It can't hurt to give the lobbyists a hearing and perhaps satisfaction – such a favour could turn into a solid stepping stone to a new job. Also, since 1996, former British military officers have 'secured over 3,500 jobs in arms and defence related companies'. This seems to be one good reason for pushing hugely expensive defence contracts through the bureaucracy, even though the company concerned may not even deliver quality products to the military.

If all else fails, spy. Infiltrate the organization that you fear may be doing you harm. Private company spying on activist groups and non-profit organizations has become another booming twenty-first-century business, raking in about $50 billion yearly – although this figure is largely due to official agencies such as the CIA or the NSA outsourcing surveillance work they used to do themselves.[15]

But spying on behalf of TNCs is flourishing as well. Much corporate spying is dealt with in-house and most major companies have a chief corporate security officer tasked with assessing and mitigating 'threats' of all sorts. Companies are naturally keen to prevent leaks of proprietary information useful to rivals, but also to avoid bad publicity and protect their brands. According to Ruskin's *Spooky Business* report, which concentrates mostly on the USA, their targets include 'environmental, anti-war, public interest, consumer, food safety, pesticide reform, nursing home reform, gun control, social justice, animal rights and arms control non-profit groups'. Walmart, Ruskin writes, is probably the most advanced American corporate spy-master, and has built in-house a kind of 'miniature CIA'.

Europe, however, hasn't been immune. Greenpeace France was a victim of spying (hacking, theft, etc.) organized by Electricité de France (EDF), the largest source of nuclear energy in the country – 75–80 per cent of French energy consumption is still fed by nuclear reactors. Guerrilla warfare between Greenpeace and France's nuclear establishment has a long history and in 1985 had tragic consequences when the *Rainbow Warrior* was blown up and sunk by the French secret services in Auckland harbour to prevent it from going to Mururoa and interfering with the planned nuclear testing. The Greenpeace photographer Fernando Pereira was killed by the second blast; 10 other crew members who had returned to the ship after the first blast narrowly escaped, because the explosion blew them into the water. The *Rainbow Warrior* caused a huge scandal in France: several people were arrested and the defence minister lost his job.[16] It was therefore immensely satisfying for many environmentalists to witness, in November 2011, EDF being fined €1.5 million and ordered to pay Greenpeace an additional €500.000 in damages. (Full disclosure: I was on the boards of Greenpeace International and Greenpeace France in the early 1990s and this outcome was indeed personally satisfying to me. The campaigns director Yannick Jadot, whose hard disk EDF hacked and copied, is now an MEP for the Greens.)

Here's another personal story, this one about corporate spying and infiltration. In 2004, Attac Switzerland published a book entitled *Attac contre l'Empire Nestlé* (Attac against Nestlé's Empire) for which they asked me, as honorary President of Attac France, to provide a preface. I did so with pleasure – the book was 150 pages long, solidly researched and gave a good account of Nestlé's influence and borderline practices worldwide. Then

I thought no more about it until Swiss French-speaking national television aired a broadcast in June 2008 asserting and demonstrating that Nestlé had infiltrated the group of Attac authors using the security firm Securitas to plant a young woman spy, 'Sara Meylan', inside the group.

Attac now has 16 national branches in Europe as well as several others in Latin America, Africa and Quebec, and calls itself an 'organization for popular education turned towards action'.[17] We have launched several campaigns to promote a financial transaction tax, close down tax havens, denounce the casino economy, fight European austerity policies and so on. For Attac-Switzerland, taking on one of the world's largest transnational corporations was all in a day's work. Any of our national organizations would be child's play to infiltrate – you just sign up as a member and take your pick of the activities you want to pursue. No one is going to doubt your *bona fides* as a starting point. So the girl who called herself 'Sara Meylan' might have been seen as a bit out of the ordinary as members go, but that would have been put down to her political naivety or some other charitable explanation. She became a member of the group working on the book.

As soon as the TV programme was broadcast, Attac-Switzerland decided to take Nestlé to court and filed a suit bringing both criminal and civil charges against the company for invasion of privacy, violation of the law for the protection of data and a couple of other motives. I joined the suit out of solidarity and because my name, after all, was on the front of the book. I also wanted to be part of the complaint because I had already had occasion to 'appreciate' Nestlé's duplicity when I wrote about its marketing of baby foods to poor mothers in poor countries and joined the campaign to stop the companies getting mothers trapped into buying breast milk substitutes. (There was nothing wrong with the powdered milk itself, but the women, once hooked, couldn't afford to continue, and overdiluted the milk with dirty water; their babies were suffering from diarrhoea or worse and meanwhile their breast milk had dried up. The companies used nurses and clinic personnel to hand out free samples.)

In 2009, the first verdict in the Swiss criminal court was handed down – after a cursory investigation based almost exclusively on Nestlé's own declarations. We lost.[18] Finally, after a long delay, the civil suit was heard in January 2012 and I went to Lausanne to testify. The big surprise there was the sudden apparition of 'Sara Meylan' herself, disguised, according to my Swiss friends, beyond recognition – with new punk hair and heavy make-up, but testimony highly favourable to our cause.

Exactly a year after that trial and four and a half years since we had filed the initial complaint, we won! Both Nestlé and Securitas were found guilty of spying and illicit infiltration. The court recognized that our rights had been violated. Nestlé and Securitas were ordered to pay each of the parties to the lawsuit 3,000 Swiss francs in 'moral reparations'. I gave back part of my award to the cause, but not all of it and confess I took enormous pleasure in spending Nestlé's money.

MEGA-LOBBIES – SORRY – 'INSTITUTES', 'COUNCILS', 'CENTRES' AND 'FOUNDATIONS'

Less well known than individual lobbyists for particular companies are the large and increasing numbers of sector-wide organizations that represent the interests of entire industries in which TNCs band together, define their goals and policies in common and share the expenses. The actions of individual corporations attract headlines because everyone has heard of them and they are 'news'. However, these individual lobby payers and players may be ultimately less dangerous than the proliferating industry-wide entities which are, in my view, more interesting because more sophisticated in their methods.

They are also more subtle, starting with their names, always along the lines of 'institutes', 'centres', 'foundations', 'councils' and the like. They are to be found mainly where laws are made – i.e., Washington, DC or Brussels, although some have worldwide regional offices. They too defend alcohol, tobacco, junk food, GMOs, chemicals and so on, but they go about it differently, with ideological weapons and well-honed training in semantics, sociology, subterfuge and science – at least enough to distort the latter, often convincingly enough to get what they want.

Corporate interests know that these institutions are vital, because they serve as plausible 'front' organizations and they understand that if a corporation or business organization is identified as the source of information, people, on the whole, won't believe it. They need a veneer which lends them respectability. These institutions and their corporate funders are investing in the future and the longer term.

FOXES AND HENS, SHEEP AND WOLVES: A EUROPEAN EXAMPLE

José Bové, a lavishly moustachioed former sheep farmer, is well known in France for his activism in all things agricultural, including opposition to GMOs and the patenting of life forms. He spent several months in prison for illegally 'harvesting' GMO crops.[19]

Since 2009, as a Green MEP, re-elected to a second five-year term in 2014, Bové has extended his range to the intricacies of Europe's workings and his tough-minded political positions to neighbouring areas including shale-gas, biotechnologies and the Transatlantic Trade and Investment Partnership (TTIP), about which you will soon read more here.

Bové has also found the time to co-author *Hold-Up à Bruxelles*,[20] full of colourful on-the-scene and backstage details about the sinister doings of shady lobbyists in the EU capital. Some European farmers may have grown accustomed to the gradual corporate takeover of our food and of nature in general – not Bové, who used to sell his sheep's milk to makers of Roquefort cheese in the Larzac, an austerely beautiful region of France where sheep, thistles and resolute farmers are about the only creatures that seem to thrive.

In his book, he shows that the mega-lobbies of the EU can be just as dangerous as those of the USA. They are the ultimate foxes in hen-houses, wolves in the sheepfold and have infiltrated – as he puts it in his subtitle – the 'heart of Europe'. Corporate personnel or lobbyists for collective, industry-wide interests have been placed in high staff positions in the official agencies whose job is to regulate those same industries. Why bother with an impartial, independent regulator when you can buy one guaranteed to make decisions in your favour?

Bové's tales of the dirty underside of European food and agricultural regulation show that the rot is pervasive in the EU. Although he is careful not to indict anyone by name if he can't prove their guilt without a doubt, it's clear that complicity with the corporations exists at the 'highest level'. This euphemism is usually enough to protect authors from libel suits.[21]

The European Food Safety Authority (EFSA) – and what Bové, with the help of his parliamentary assistants, managed almost single-handedly to do about it – is a modern morality tale. First of all, surveys year after year show that two-thirds to three-quarters of Europeans don't want GMOs on their plates and want those that are for sale labelled. Even if, like many Americans, you argue that there is no scientific basis for refusing to eat GMO products, their negative environmental impact is well documented for a number of crops and species such as butterflies. Furthermore, it's economic folly to allow a natural resource as important as seeds to come under the exclusive control of a handful of huge corporations, in this case principally

Monsanto, Bayer and Syngenta. Monopolies always behave like monopolies, and for that reason industrialized countries have enacted laws against them for at least a century. Today, they also come together for reasons other than just crude price fixing or restricting markets.

The EU is a work-in-progress. It had, for example, no food safety agency until 2002 after a series of disasters, including 'mad cow disease' (bovine spongiform encephalitis), the 'pig plague' (porcine epidemic diarrhoea virus) and various other unappetizing outbreaks, forced the EU to act by creating the EFSA, located in Parma, Italy. EFSA's main initial mission was to harmonize the rules developed by the then 15 member countries, mostly because the Commission was anxious to ensure that its notorious 'free and unhindered competition' rules extended to foodstuffs as well as other goods and services. Most Europeans understandably don't care to risk eating poison pork chops or importing diseased animals whose meat and milk could infect them with Creutzfeldt-Jacob disease. The EFSA thus also inherited the job of regulating and verifying the safety of GMOs in food.

When John Dalli, the European Commissioner for Health and Consumers,[22] gave the green light to a GMO potato called Amflora, developed by the German chemicals giant BASF, Bové went into red alert mode. His first stop was EFSA. Dalli in his former life was an accountant; he had no scientific background and was relying on EFSA to give him its recommendations. What sort of tests, Bové wanted to know, had been run on this high-starch potato intended not so much for people as for the paper and adhesives industries that buy starch as a raw material? Did EFSA realize that a 'marker gene' resistant to antibiotics had been introduced into this new potato whose shoots would be left in fields and could be easily transmitted to other potatoes for human consumption? Did they realize that the by-products of starch production are often used as animal feed?

Bové carried a concealed weapon. He had discovered that the president of EFSA, Diana Banati, the top official who decided which scientists and what studies would be involved in the authorization procedure, was also a member of the Board of the International Life Sciences Institute (ILSI). And what was the ILSI? None other than the world's largest mega-lobby in the food and health sector, dealing with toxicology, food safety, the environment, nutrition, risk assessment and so on. Founded in 1978 (the European branch in the 1980s) and based in Washington, ILSI is made up of 62 industrial giants including BASF – the inventor of the new potato – Bayer, Monsanto; grain-trade giants Cargill and Bunge; Coca-Cola, Pepsi and Red Bull; Danone, General Mills, Kellogg, Nestlé, McDonald's Europe, Unilever and pharmaceutical manufacturers Pfizer, Johnson & Johnson, Merck, Sanofi-Aventis, Syngenta, Dow Chemical – the list goes on.

Before taking on the presidency of EFSA, Banati had not seen fit to inform any of the EU political authorities of her links to ILSI. Bové and his team informed her that they would allow two months for her to do so. Her conflict of interest had to be made public. Nothing happened. Bové called a press conference to take place on the day he had set as the deadline and decided that he would announce the conflict of interest himself. Banati had had fair warning.

A few hours before meeting the press, Bové and his assistants took a final look at the relevant EFSA site and were rewarded by an 'Aha!' moment. Banati had indeed declared her conflict of interest to EFSA – less than 48 hours before the press conference was scheduled to begin. Here was a clear admission of guilt and, meanwhile, Bové's team of parliamentary assistants had also discovered that a great many other ILSI company staff scientists were to be found in other EU regulatory agencies such as EMA and ECHA, charged with pharmaceuticals and chemicals regulations.[23]

These connections reflect the common Brussels practice of the 'revolving door' – switching from a regulatory agency, EU Commission or parliamentary job to a company; or, in the case of the ILSI corporate scientists, vice-versa – perhaps placed in key positions in the regulatory agencies by their former employers as useful plants for the future. In Banati's case, the door didn't revolve – she was EFSA's top staff member and a board member of ILSI simultaneously. Even when working over-time, the revolving door is still not adequately guarded despite numerous examples of top personnel gliding immediately and without friction from a civil servant or political existence to a lucrative position in the private sector – often as a lobbyist.

Bové's description of his investigations of chemicals and pharma agencies stops in 2012. Examining their websites two years on, it looked to me as though both were trying to make sensible rules against conflicts of interest and to protect their reputations. The tightening up may well have been prompted by his activity. Both agencies, however, are of necessity in constant contact with the industries whose products they are evaluating. They ought to be under the scrutiny of independent citizens' watchdog panels that could set boundaries and warn of possible missteps.

ILSI's political connections seem to me to require further examination, which can only be undertaken by people with some status and clout, such as MEPs. Am I paranoid to find suspicious that in mid-2014, the wholly corporate-operated and corporate-funded ILSI was carrying out seven scientific studies commissioned by, and receiving funding from, the EU? The EU is paying out a total of nearly €42 million for this work, which cannot help but have an impact on the decisions taken by the EFSA. They concern such subjects as 'food allergen and allergy risk management' or 'total diet study exposure', including consumer exposure to contaminants such as 'heavy metals, mycotoxins or organic pollutants'. There's also one on 'drug-resistant bacteria and transfer of antimicrobial resistance throughout the food chain' budgeted at €9 million. You may recall that resistance to antibiotics was one of the contentious points for BASF's super-starch Amflora potato. Are the hens in the EU directorates commissioning studies by the foxes?

Surely, many qualified university labs could do this work, but then they would have to jump through all the hoops of the Research Directorate, finding partners in several countries and submitting endless forms. Many highly qualified labs have either hired a person full time to deal with the EU research bureaucracy's demands or have decided not to waste time and money in pursuing the contracts. I would be very interested to see the hundreds of pages that I am sure the ILSI was required to fill out. Or might it have been exempt?

EU parliamentarians and anti-lobbying organizations ought to follow the matter closely, since it could be a scenario for future conflicts of interest. Or are we to trust implicitly the evaluations and assessments carried out by the scientists of an entirely corporate entity such as ILSI? Can they be counted on to treat vital questions concerning food safety impartially? Who, if anyone, will have the power to judge their judgements?

And just offhand, what's happened to that super-starch potato? BASF was miffed that consumers, farmers and political decision-makers refused to give its new transgenic potato a warm reception and announced in 2012 that, first, it would no longer develop this particular variety and, second, in any case was moving its entire transgenic research shop to the United States. BASF escaped just in time: in 2013, the European Court of Justice handed down its decision invalidating the authorization given the Amflora potato by the European Commission, a well-deserved slap in the face.

And what of Diana 'Conflict of Interest' Banati? Not to worry: she too has floated effortlessly from being president of EFSA to taking the top staff job at – you guessed it – ILSI, the very International Life Sciences Institute from which she had been obliged to resign after lying to EFSA about her connection to it. Today she is ILSI's executive and scientific director. The well-oiled revolving door seems to be spinning at a good clip and we may note in passing that the lobbying machine takes good care of its own.

A MODERN METAMORPHOSIS: THE IASB

This section isn't about an actual lobby, but touches on the journey that corporate interests can make to officialdom, another way of taking over public interest jurisdiction. It concerns the International Accounting Standards Board (IASB) and its parent, the International Financial Reporting Standards Foundation. Never heard of them? You aren't supposed to have heard of them, you and 99-plus per cent of the rest of the European population. They make up one of those 'purely technical' organizations – a little like a European regulatory body, except that they, not elected legislators, make the accounting rules, not just for Europe but well beyond. And anyway, isn't accounting the most boring subject on earth, unless you're an accountant or someone who is professionally obliged to follow its standards? Why should we care who makes the rules?

Not so fast! The story is more interesting than that. When the EU was first confronted around 2001 with enlargement and the nightmare of more than 20 different stock exchanges, sets of regulations and company accounting rules, it called on an ad hoc group of advisers from the big four transnational accounting firms for help.[24] Over the following years, this informal advisory group quietly morphed into an official one with an iron-clad structure.

The foundation that encompasses the IASB is not-for-profit and contains two subunits – the IASB, still made up primarily of talent from the big four accountancy firms, and the foundation's

Interpretation Committee made up of 14 voting members who are 'aware of the current issues as they arise and [possess] the technical ability to resolve them'. These two spaces are where the action takes place; they are overseen by the foundation's trustees and its monitoring board charged with ensuring public accountability.

The IASB became official through the unrelenting efforts of a single unelected EU commissioner, Charlie MacCreevy, a fervently neoliberal Irishman, himself a chartered accountant. There was no parliamentary review. If any legislator or citizens' body thought to ask, they were given the standard put-off: the agency was 'purely technical'. And indeed, what could be more tediously technical than accounting rules and practices? Again, who cares?

Let me make clear that I do not for a moment question the technical competence of the people making up these different elements of this complex structure. My problem, and I believe our common one, stems from what looks like a planned incapacity to think anywhere outside an extremely narrow box, and for some of those in charge, this can only be deliberate. The IASB and the interpretations committee have the capacity and the conscious or unconscious incentive to preserve the status quo and tailor the agenda to whatever system is most congenial to the big four accounting firms themselves, plus the TNC corporate clients whose accounts they help define and audit and whose tax advising and planning they may well do in addition. Their ability to limit the horizon in the era of financial globalization is detrimental to all the citizens of all the countries that are obliged to follow IASB rules and to accept the interpretation committee's decisions, because they are the only game in town.

In practice, this includes all the citizens of all the member countries of the EU, as well as those of Argentina, Australia, Brazil, Canada, Mexico, Korea, Russia, Saudi Arabia, South Africa and Turkey, plus those of countries where 'convergence' is in process. China ('substantially converged standards'), India and Indonesia are on that list, with Japan a bit lower down. As usual, the USA has been, and will remain, the main hold-out.

We should care that the IASB is deciding the rules for Europe, the BRICS and many other developing countries, because unless and until we can oblige TNCs to adopt country-by-country accountancy and tax reporting, they will continue to pay – quite legally – minimal taxes in most of the countries where they have branches. They can practise 'transfer pricing', which allows the company to buy and sell from itself at whatever price best suits its purpose and to play with national tax rules.

According to an expert at the OECD, 60 per cent or more of international 'trade' takes place between subsidiaries of a parent transnational corporation that can charge each other whatever is convenient. Profits are situated in low or no-tax jurisdictions and losses in high-tax ones. They can make maximum use of the world's ample supply of tax havens and, in a word, rob countries blind of the taxes actually owed them.[25]

Here is an example provided by the Tax Justice Network, except that I've changed the names. Company *TNC* produces a t-shirt at a cost of €10 and sells it to its subsidiary *CozyTaxHaven* for €10. *TNC* pays no tax, since it made no profit. *CozyTaxHaven* sells the shirt to *TNC-Distribution* for €20. *CozyTaxHaven* makes a profit of €10 but pays no tax because the government where it is registered doesn't levy one. *TNC-Distribution* sells the t-shirt for €15 to the final customer at a loss of €5. But *TNC* mother company makes €5 tax free (and maybe gets some subsidies from the government in addition). This simplified example shows how easy it is to manipulate prices, contribute nothing to one's home country's treasury and remain perfectly legal.[26] It's just as easy to manipulate services by using other intra-company accounting tricks such as putting your marketing or publicity expenditures wherever it suits you.

A report by two French parliamentarians, Alain Bocquet

and Nicolas Dupont-Aignan, to the National Assembly Foreign Affairs Committee estimates the losses to France in unpaid corporate taxes at somewhere between €60 and €80 billion a year compared to total actual corporate taxation receipts, in 2013, of €53 billion. Even if the lower figure – a shortfall of €60 billion – is chosen, France could more than double its 2013 revenue from corporate taxes.[27] The authors provide a tableau of just five high-flyer American TNCs – Google, Apple, Facebook, Amazon and Microsoft – which together declared a sales figure for France far lower than it actually was, according to the authors. These same companies ought to have paid 22 times more in French taxes than they did.

Meanwhile, while citizens are being told to tighten their belts, pay higher income tax and VAT and consent to austerity measures, corporations will have received in 2014 the manna from heaven of tens of billions of euros in lower social charges.

And that's just the corporate tax. Value-added tax throughout the EU also shows steep shortfalls, with France and Italy the biggest losers at €36 and €32 billion of VAT going uncollected. In 2012, the EU estimated total losses to tax fraud and evasion at a cool trillion. The French authors of the parliamentary report say it's double that. Nobody really knows how much it is, except that it's a lot and that European citizens could also be a lot better off and contribute far more to the general welfare of the world if they weren't handing over such colossal sums yearly to the banks and the TNCs.

To tax effectively, fiscal authorities would need to know what the figures for sales, expenditures, profits and taxes actually are in each national jurisdiction. That is the goal of country-by-country reporting. Today, they cannot find out, because the accounting rules are designed to avoid disclosure. Small businesses limited to a single country and families with a fixed national address will continue to bear most of the tax burden or their country will simply do without the state services that fair taxation of TNCs could have provided.

We know the sovereign remedy for tax evasion: it's country-by-country reporting. It wouldn't totally solve the problem, but corporations couldn't get away with lying to everyone. Now they need only declare sales and profits in their headquarters country and make one entry for 'Rest of World'. The Tax Justice Network has all the details and its chartered accountant adviser Richard Murphy has been championing country-by-country reporting for years. Murphy likes to say that the transnationals ought to be considered for the prestigious literary Booker Prize because their accounts are works of fiction.

Is the IASB worrying about this mammoth problem, which is stealing countless billions from Europe and other member countries? All I could find on its site was this:

> Before it started the public consultation [which took place in 2011] the IASB was asked to consider introducing country-by-country reporting requirements. The agenda consultation revealed little support for such a project and we do not plan to undertake any specific work on this topic.[28]

To make absolutely sure there was nothing planned on this vital subject, I contacted the IASB in mid-2013 to ask if country-by-country reporting was anywhere on their agenda and received a polite reply that it was not. No wonder. The big four firms whose friends and colleagues make the rules would lose millions in revenue if they could no longer advise their clients on how best to avoid taxation. Their corporate clients would not be amused if they could no longer under-declare and underpay their taxes in each jurisdiction while making abundant use of tax havens.

So as is the usual story with the TNCs: everyone wins except that negligible quantity – the citizens.

RICHARD BERMAN *LE MAGNIFIQUE*

A man the US lobbying establishment looks up to as a living legend is Richard Berman, creator of many mega-lobbies and an accomplished public relations guru who also holds a law degree. Berman's Tobacco Institute, for example, was able to put off binding legislation on tobacco for years, including non-smoking areas in restaurants. Corporate clients can't ask for more. Although the science may be blindingly clear and lung cancer visibly lethal, creating doubt in the public mind is usually sufficient to stave off the lawmakers. Berman has defended the alcoholic beverage and junk food industries as well as preparing anti-union campaigns for large corporations. Now in his early seventies, he still runs such non-profit outfits as the American Beverage Institute and the Center for Consumer Freedom, dealing with 'food, beverage and life-style issues'.

Berman's Center for Union Facts and the Employment Policies Institute are both profoundly anti-labour. Name a contentious issue on which any legislative changes could reduce industry profits – obesity, GMOs, fizzy drinks, smoking, taxes, alcohol consumption, labour laws and the minimum wage – Berman has worked on it and always – it goes without saying – on behalf of corporations that want no changes. He argued successfully, for example, that raising the minimum wage would reduce employment, particularly for the poor and uneducated and he was a consultant to, if not the creator of, the Minimum Wage Coalition to Save Jobs. Not for nothing have labour activists labelled him 'Dr Evil'.

The many entities he has founded all have ingratiating and positive-sounding names and all of them are non-profit organizations. Berman's services, however, are so highly valued that his industry donors don't mind if huge portions of the 'donations' they give to his non-profit creations go straight to Berman and Company, of which he is sole owner and executive director.

Berman and Company is definitely a profit-making business. The Center for Consumer Freedom in 2008 sent this company 93 per cent of the donations it received; the Beverages Institute handed over 82 per cent of its haul. Berman serves on the boards of both. It's a neat way for businesses to pay for commercial services.

So far, the tax people don't seem to mind either, although private individuals and for-profit companies like Berman's are not supposed to profit from 'charities' or 'educational' organizations like the ones he has set up. His earnings from these sham 'institutes' et al. are in the millions. Without Berman, Americans would not have learned that labour unions are harmful to workers, that consumers' freedom means people have the right to drink as much alcohol ('social drinking') and eat as much rubbish as they like or that the Humane Society is a threat to animals.[29] Berman's donors have included Coca-Cola, Philip Morris, alcoholic beverages manufacturers and a great many American restaurant chains.[30]

I can't swear that Berman actually invented the genre of the mega-lobby, but his example has not gone unnoticed.

WHO'S BOOZE BLUES

The World Health Organization (WHO), has a drinking problem. In the 20 years between 1990 and 2010, alcohol consumption went from rank number six to number three on the WHO *Global Burden of Disease* chart.[31] WHO estimates that harmful drinking kills 2.5 million people a year compared to about half that many who die in road accidents. Only high blood pressure and tobacco contribute more to ill health and premature death.

The alcohol industry sells a trillion dollars' worth of booze a year and it's not making the mistake of the tobacco industry, which denied the scientific evidence for as long as it could.[32] The drinks-makers recommend personal restraint or 'responsible drinking', no advertisements targeting minors and 'corporate social responsibility'. The instrument it uses to promote its solutions is the International Center for Alcohol Policies (ICAP). I hope you felt a sudden twinge of suspicion just reading the name, and wonder who funds ICAP. Answer: some of the world's major alcoholic beverages firms.

There is plenty of evidence in favour of lowering alcohol consumption rates and it shows that higher prices, restricted availability and banning advertising are the way to go. There's also plenty of evidence that the policies recommended by ICAP don't work. ICAP uses tried and true lobbying techniques – downplay the science and say that there is debate among the people who produce it when in fact there isn't. And never address your adversaries' arguments, such as the three just cited.

The newest strategy is using social media; Diageo credited its 'multimillion strategic partnership' with Facebook for increasing sales of five key brands by 20 per cent. Experts like the professor of social marketing at the University of Stirling, quoted in the *New Scientist*, know that '[i]t's infinitely more powerful for a message to come from your mate than from Diageo'.

There's no reason for the corporations to want to discourage heavy drinking when the heaviest drinking 10 per cent of the population consumes 45–55 per cent of all the alcohol sold. They've also found a virgin market in developing countries where huge cohorts of possible future young drinkers are coming of age. The journal *Addiction* published the conclusions of two Norwegian researchers who had studied the draft alcohol policies of four African countries and noted that they were remarkably similar and closely aligned with ICAP's recommendations. Delving further into the electronic evidence, they were able to establish that the 'author' of the policies was the policy and issues manager of one of the major TNC brewers and sponsors of ICAP.

Raising the cost of drinking works. So does lowering it: in Scotland, where consumption has doubled in the past 50 years as prices fell and availability increased, the public health costs of alcohol-related diseases have reached £3.6 billion a year – for a country of 5.25 million people. As ICAP continues to set policy and the disease burden of alcohol climbs worldwide, it look as though millions who've never been to Scotland will join in singing 'We'll take a cup o' kindness yet for Auld Lang Syne'.

THE WORLD'S WORST PROBLEM: CLIMATE CHANGE

The time has come to describe the greatest lobbying triumph of all time – as well as the most evil and the most anti-democratic. Financial collapse engineered by the deregulation of banks and the insatiability of their leadership seems almost trivial compared to the wilful deregulation of the earth's systems, pushing nameless billions to the brink of survival and perhaps beyond. We are all trapped in the building where the flames are crackling at the base; we are all frogs in the water whose temperature is going up ever so gradually.

Crimes against our only home cannot be prosecuted. The corporations paying for earth's ruin cannot, so far, be touched. For the thorniest, most controversial, most devastating challenges faced by humanity, the forces promoting them have invented far more sophisticated, durable and costly structures than those outlined in this chapter. They are placed in the service of an enormously successful climate change denialists' movement.[33]

A combination of think-tanks, conservative foundations, personnel skilled in lobbying and truly astonishing amounts of money have slowed down and perhaps doomed the genuine efforts made by millions of people to halt and reverse climate change. The corporations paying for all this should in my view be charged with crimes against humanity, but that cannot happen in today's United States.

After the failure of the UN Copenhagen climate conference in 2009, one denialist coalition funded by the petroleum and motor industries even announced on their site that they were disbanding, considering that they had accomplished their purpose. And in many ways they had. The industry is thriving, there is far less media coverage and, at least in the United States, lower public concern about climate change than before 2009.

Dr Robert Brulle, professor of sociology and environmental science at Drexel University in Philadelphia, has published a study on the climate change denialist movement and explicitly on how it is funded. His conclusions are shattering. Having developed a list of 118 denialist organizations in the United States, he then collected data on the sources of funding for each one. It will surprise no one that the largest and most consistent funders were a good number of neoconservative or libertarian foundations with close ties to TNCs that were promoting 'ultra-free-market ideas' in many areas. Brulle found that between 2003 and 2010, 140 foundations had channelled $558 million to about 100 climate change denialist organizations. You can buy a lot of pseudo-science, *ad hominem* attacks and propaganda with more than half a billion dollars.

Since 2010, when Brulle's data collection stops, the funders have grown much more secretive, cautious and clever in masking their donations. Brulle found that prior to 2008 the ExxonMobil Foundation and the Koch Affiliated Foundations were 'heavily involved' in funding climate change denial, but since then contributions from both have 'dramatically declined'.

Really? Don't count on it. Grants probably stayed level or even increased, but since they can be channelled anonymously through special-purpose and ideologically determined financial vehicles such as Donors Capital Fund or Donors Trust, they need not admit to this funding. The proof is that simultaneously with this 'dramatic decline', these sister organizations had somehow managed an equally dramatic rise in their contributions.

As the Donors Capital Fund proudly announces, when you have an account with Donors Trust, 'you save money, gain complete anonymity, and secure your philanthropy legacy for the principles of freedom'. Anything in your account is imme-diately tax-deductible even before you have given away a single dollar. The 'complete anonymity' is a great selling point and surely many private foundations of any size, as well as corporate donors, have happily handed over their funds to someone who will send their money exactly where they want it to go with no hassle.

Giving through a donor's account also avoids delicate family issues after you have gone to your eternal reward in capitalist heaven. For example, if your children don't agree with your ultra-right-wing ideas and want to give the money still in your account to progressive organizations, they can't. Donors Trust knows that, even dead, you remain anti-government and pro-free market – otherwise they wouldn't have let you in to begin with. It has its own lists of all the OK organizations you would have approved and will make sure your heirs sign on the dotted line.

The huge foundations, such as those of the Koch brothers and ExxonMobil, are probably most interested in 'complete anonymity'. Brulle reports that Donors Trust alone now accounts for at least 25 per cent of all traceable contributions to denialist organizations. The donors themselves are not trace-able; their accounts can't be violated because all the money leaving Donors Trust on behalf of its account holders is going to 'charities' that are tax-deductible. It's a neat concept.[34]

The climate denial industry takes us well beyond mere lob-bying or even conspiracy, although it has elements of both. It is the ultimate challenge to democracy because it promotes false information and makes sure that enough citizens are confused

– or at least confused enough to doubt the enormous threat on which the real science is perfectly clear. Peoples' lives and those of their children may hang in the balance, but they are uninformed, ignorant and kept comfortable that way. The Republican Party recognizes that it is political suicide to run candidates who affirm a belief in climate change.

These donations from the Koch brothers (oil and gas), ExxonMobil and all the others are trying to ensure that the world uses every drop of fossil fuel still hiding under land or sea. Unless a sea change in US politics occurs, these people will never have criminal charges levied against them. Citizens of other countries than the USA have no power to stop the flood of funds that keeps the denialist institutions in business and the misinformation flowing freely, even though it is the future of the entire world and of all its inhabitants that is at stake.

Not only do a few billionaires and their corporations have incalculably more money and power than everyone else on earth, but they have seized the right to place their immediate profit above the future of humankind. Climate change is no longer an issue affecting only 'future generations' – generations on earth today will suffer the consequences. The poorer and more vulnerable they are today, the more they will suffer tomorrow. In present law, no crime has been committed, despite the rising numbers of climate refugees seeking shelter and the victims of drought and floods. These are not natural but unnatural disasters, and they are on the increase.

Crimes against the earth and her people cannot be punished. Acts of universal malice are ignored and their perpetrators go free: the dimensions of the wrongdoing are unfathomable for our inadequate security systems that cannot take in the scope of the problem. We desperately need enforceable laws that can prevent corporations from destroying democracy, human rights and life itself.

2

TRANSNATIONAL TREATIES: TAILORED BY AND FOR TRANSNATIONAL CORPORATIONS

In business, it's smart to stand on the right side of the law, but even smarter to make the law yourself so you can stand where you like.[1] Understanding this, the transnationals have crafted an expedient and enduring bargain with governments – the latter growing more amenable and the former more insatiable with each passing year.

Writing the legislation in the interests of particular companies or industries is a lobbyist's bread and butter, but actually determining government policy in an area worth hundreds of billions annually – now *that's* influence. Doing so on an international scale takes the gold. TNCs began working in this direction as soon as twentieth-century globalization got under way and their maiden voyage took place in 1986 when governments came together in the Uruguay Round to negotiate the creation of a World Trade Organization (WTO).

SOME HISTORY: FIRST STEPS TO A TAKEOVER

The WTO was a hugely ambitious undertaking. Before its existence, only trade in goods was governed by the international rules developed by the General Agreement on Tariffs and Trade (GATT) signed in 1947. The Uruguay Round, one of a series, used the GATT as a starting point and kept all its rules, but its purpose was to add services, agriculture, government procurement, intellectual property and investment, as well as many new regulations, for example those pertaining to health and plant safety.[2] Despite trade union pressure, no labour or social chapters were included. The negotiators took nearly a decade to agree on a deal but by 1994, governments were ready to sign and the WTO was officially launched in Marrakech and began work in Geneva on 1 January 1995. By 2014 it had 160 members.

In 1947 when the GATT was born, it's doubtful there was a particular lobbying push by business – at least I've found no evidence of one – and the frontiers between government and business were pretty well defined. By the time negotiations on the WTO had begun 40 years later, those frontiers had grown far more porous. TNCs crossed them with ease, touting their own priorities. As David Hartridge, then Director of the WTO Services Division, later remarked:

> Without the enormous pressures exerted by the American financial sector, particularly companies like American Express and Citicorp, there would have been no GATS [General Agreement on Trade in Services] and therefore perhaps no Uruguay Round and no WTO ... The US fought to get services on the agenda and they were right.[3]

'Enormous pressure' – and the USA 'fighting' to obtain agreement from every other country – ensured that the WTO agreement was full of goodies for the TNCs and gave them access to huge new areas. The entertainment and film industries were also said to be particularly active. The honeymoon stage didn't last long, however. Both the companies and their home governments quickly became frustrated by the slow pace of change. The WTO was set up as a 'permanent negotiating forum'; it was supposed to provide a non-stop avenue to further trade liberalization – but it got hopelessly bogged down.

A dozen years after it began, the so-called Doha Round, launched in November 2001 in the post-9/11 war-on-terror fervour that blanketed the world, was still nowhere near completion. The Bali ministerial meeting in late 2013 claimed great advances, but many participants found these claims just as overblown as those made in previous years, which had led nowhere.

The WTO 'judiciary' – or Dispute Resolution Mechanism – allowing one member country to make complaints against the trade policies or misdeeds of another, was actually quite speedy as such things go, but could still cause long delays. As for the negotiations proper, according to WTO rules, nothing is agreed until everything is agreed so members could and did go on bickering about this or that issue – often agriculture – for years on end. The spectacle of constant squabbling and the glacial speed of further liberalization inspired richer countries in particular to stop hanging around waiting for some 150 nations to get down to business and agree on anything. Pascal Lamy, previously the European trade commissioner, would doubtless reject nomination for sainthood, but it must have taken the patience of one to endure two four-year terms as Director-General of WTO (from 1 September 2005 to 31 August 2013), during which time virtually nothing memorable happened.

To keep things moving in the direction they wanted, and in the absence of worldwide agreement on anything, the powerful countries set out aggressively to recruit partners for bilateral and regional free trade agreements (FTAs), routinely combined with the provisions of bilateral investment treaties (BITs), although these could also be signed separately. WTO members wasted no time: according to Lamy, speaking in late 2012, 'we can count almost 400 preferential trade agreements currently in existence, and each member of the WTO on average belongs to 13 separate agreements'.[4]

What are the motivations – not just of the more powerful but also of the weaker states to sign these agreements? Again, let's turn to Lamy, who had plenty of time to reflect on the matter while the Doha Round was getting nowhere.

> A number of reasons can be adduced to explain [the agree-ments] rising and continuing. They may serve political or strategic ends. Countries may wish to go further and faster in the direction of economic integration than they have been able to do in the WTO. They may be motivated by a fear of exclu-sion as competing countries secure better access to markets of interest. They may be an insurance policy against future protectionism. They may act as a signalling device to attract foreign investment. They may also serve as a vehicle for policy consolidation nationally, using an international obligation to make it harder for domestic interests to exert an influence over trade policy.[5]

So depending on national power status, adversaries and per-ceived interests, a government can have lots of reasons to accept such treaties. Nonetheless, and whatever the hoped-for benefits, they shouldn't sign up without full recognition of the downsides, as many have learned to their cost.

Protection and privileges for their investors were also important to the more powerful countries. According to the UN Conference on Trade and Development (UNCTAD), by mid-2013 nearly 3,200 BITs were in force. All of them are necessarily 'WTO-plus', meaning that they open up to their partners new areas for investment (for example, via government procurement) and extend new rights to TNC investors.

International treaties are an important source of law. Some provisions, when included again and again, come to be called 'customary law'. More formally, at least for the 66 countries that have signed and ratified the Vienna Convention of the Law of Treaties of 1969, treaty provisions always – at least theoretically – outrank national law, including constitutions. Signatories of the Vienna convention include a great many states in Africa, Central and South America and Asia. Among the most important are China, the USSR (as it then was), Brazil, Australia, Canada, the United Kingdom and South Korea. The USA signed but has never ratified the Vienna convention, whereas nearly all the Eastern and Western European countries, including the UK and Germany, have done both (although France has done neither) and this has given Brussels a sound foundation on which to propose further liberalization through the use of international law.

Indeed, the EU Commission is relentlessly entrepreneurial where FTAs and BITs are concerned. So is the USA, but it has found different ways to get what it wants. One is the Investor to State Dispute Settlement (ISDS) process, which is a clever, if quite diabolical, invention that allows the TNCs themselves to make international law. We'll be looking at ISDS in detail.

In their negotiations with prospective FTA/BIT partners, both Europe and the USA invariably demand a kind of WTO-double-plus agreement and a state-of-the-art, iron-clad investment chapter. 'State of the art' means that every new treaty is expected to incorporate whatever the same partner has conceded in a previous one. Recall too that new free trade or bilateral investment treaties never contradict the WTO, but they go way beyond its rules and are registered as 'WTO compatible' with this umbrella organization. All the additions are made with the TNCs in mind and the latter have duly lobbied the governmental negotiators. Yet even as they were signing dozens of binding bilateral treaties, the biggest political players were not satisfied. They had far more grandiose ambitions.

ENTER THE ERA OF ALL-ENCOMPASSING TRADE TREATIES

In July 2013, negotiations began in Brussels on the Transatlantic Trade and Investment Partnership (TTIP), a joint agreement between the USA and Europe and the most ambitious FTA ever attempted.

This treaty, if it is approved and ratified according to the TNC's plan, may include changes to regulations covering safety and standards for food, pharmaceuticals, chemicals, GMOs, hydraulic fracturation ('fracking') and so on. It could have the final say on financial stability proposals and give freedom to investors to remove their capital without notice. It could increase the lifespan of patents and other intellectual property, making drugs and other purchases more expensive and preventing the spread of knowledge and technology. It would put pressure on wholly or partially state-owned enterprises to privatize and could conceivably block proposals for new taxes such as the financial transaction tax, prevent improvement in labour laws including wages, and reduce government capacity to deal with climate security, for example if it tried to impose higher standards on polluting industries.

The agreement applies to all levels of government; thus local, state, regional or national governments could be forbidden to give preference to local over foreign companies for procurement contracts which contribute significantly to any modern economy. The entire negotiating process will take place behind closed doors with no input from citizens, although corporations will have free access. That's the good news compared to what follows.[6]

Note, however, that I have put nearly all these statements

in the conditional tense because the negotiations are secret, even our national or European parliamentarians can't read the texts or learn what has been agreed as they go along. We can't say how much European – or for that matter American – negotiators will be prepared to give away. But all the dangers listed *could* become part of our political landscape tomorrow and we are about to see how this has come about.

THE TRADE TREATIES AND GEOPOLITICS

This chapter will cover in detail only the United States–European TTIP treaty, particularly the constant involvement of corporate interests, but a word about the political context is useful. A similar grand treaty with Asia, called the Transpacific Trade Partnership (TTP), came first, in line with the United States' well-publicized foreign policy shift from West to East known as the 'pivot to Asia'. Two years before the TTIP negotiations began in 2013, the USA and 11 other Pacific Rim countries – Australia, Brunei, Canada, Chile, Japan, Malaysia, Mexico, New Zealand, Peru, Singapore and Vietnam – had kicked off negotiations on the TTP.

By early 2014, those talks had been through several rounds and although the usual claims of great strides forward were made, they were going more slowly than the protagonists had hoped. For good reason, it seems. As a Malaysian MP explained:

> In the text of the agreement, there's only one chapter that's about trade and 24 chapters that aren't ... It's not a trade agreement but an agreement to control trade in the interests of the biggest corporations ... Where's our sovereignty? Business is regulating government.[7]

The most salient geopolitical points to make about the TTP and the TTIP are these:

- The wealth and trade relationships which the Atlantic and Pacific groups of countries embody are colossal; they come to huge shares of world GDP (nearly two-thirds) and of world trade (nearly three-quarters).[8]
- Since the USA is a member of both groups, its corporations should be the best-positioned of all.
- If either one of these treaties is adopted, it will create strong political and commercial pressure and provide compelling arguments to sign the other one. The same provisions, rules and standards will have to be included because they will represent the 'state of the art' and, indeed, the areas covered by both treaties are almost identical, represent the same commercial interests and conceal the same dangers.
- If both were signed, it would be TNC heaven: if the remaining countries – the rest of the world (ROW) – then wanted to sign a trade agreement with any of the partners to TPP or TTIP, they would almost certainly have to agree and sign on for the same obligations.
- If such a coup of the century could be brought off, the scenario for holdout governments would be Take It or Leave It: sign and accept what we say or be largely frozen out of commerce. Note that the most important BRICS economies – Brazil, Russia, India and, above all, China – do not figure in these major commercial efforts, yet even such major economies and trading partners would be put under heavy strain should they try to escape the rules made without them. Such are the power politics, giving the United States a clear path to world hegemony in a vital area while conferring junior partner status on Europe.

HOW DID THE TTIP GET STARTED?
WHO'S BEHIND IT?

Now let's see how the TTIP was designed and what it specifically holds in store – we'll be more precise on the various
sectors it covers later. By itself, this agreement would make
the rules governing some €2 billion worth of trade a day and
the economies of the two richest areas in the world. In both
predictable and unpredictable ways, it would touch the lives of
more than 800 million people, not to mention nearly everyone
in the world by one means or another.

The TTIP may only have been unveiled in 2013, but it had
been under careful preparation for decades.

As soon as the ink was dry on the document creating the
WTO in 1994, the corporations began gearing up for even
grander conquests. Within a year, according to its site, the
Transatlantic Business Dialogue (TABD) 'was convened in
1995 by the US Department of Commerce and the European
Commission to serve as the *official* [my italics] dialogue between
American and European business leaders and US cabinet secre-
taries and EU commissioners.' These governments were already
cooperating fully with the TNCs and didn't mind saying so. Duly
officialized, the 70 invited TABD member companies explained
to the politicians and bureaucrats how best to proceed, or,
as the European Commission explained in 2000, '*In line with
TABD recommendations*, we have made particular efforts in the
field of standards, certification and regulatory issues', sector by
sector.[9]

This was the first stage of USA–EU corporate lawmaking.
From the outset, the TABD set up working groups composed
of relevant industry representatives to examine 'standards
and regulatory issues' which were always front and centre in
their sights. TABD members adopted what could be called an
ambitious, not to say presumptuous, slogan: 'Approved Once,

Accepted Everywhere' – meaning 'If we – the TNCs on both sides of the pond – approve it, you had better accept it too.'

SLOGAN AS LAW

The purpose of the negotiations now under way is to make this slogan law: that is the job of government negotiators. If the treaty is then signed and ratified, it will also be up to governments to make the slogan binding and to oblige their people to swallow it. The state is still necessary, governments have their place and TNCs have no desire to govern directly, but that does not make their real authority any less illegitimate. Governments are complicit: they set up the TABD to begin with, fully intending to put the TNCs in charge of state commercial, trade and regulatory policy.

Membership of the TABD covers all the economically important sectors, including three of the 'big four' TNC accounting firms; chemical and pharmaceutical giants such as Pfizer, Merck, Lilly, BASF; several IT companies – Microsoft, Oracle, Intel; petroleum majors such as Total, Exxon and BP; German industrial heavyweights Siemens and ThyssenKrupp; tobacco firms BAT and Phillip Morris, plus what might seem a surprising number of transnational consulting groups and international law firms.

Did the TABD itself spring, so to speak, fully armed from the head of Zeus (or Jacques Delors, Commission President from 1988 to 1994)? Not at all. On the European side, it was preceded by the European Roundtable of Industrialists (ERT), founded in 1983 by 18 chief executives of major European TNCs. Today, the ERT claims that its members – the CEOs of about 50 companies – oversee an economic turnover of a trillion euros and have created 6.6 million jobs, 2.6 million of them directly, the others indirectly. These are the same TNC people who designed and promoted the EU Lisbon Strategy, which is a carbon copy of the ERT demands. These are most fully expressed in its report, *Vision for a Competitive Europe in 2025* ('with recommendations for policy actions', as it modestly says on the cover). Officialdom had only to transcribe and the ERT members have continued to put their wish lists on the table, fully expecting them to be accepted. For example, in March 2013, Chancellor Merkel of Germany invited President Hollande of France and 15 ERT CEOs to Berlin, where veteran corporation men Jean-Louis Beffa (Saint Gobain and several top industrial and bank boards) and Gerhard Cromme (Siemens, ThyssenKrupp) presented their report on 'competitivity'. The authors have been close friends for decades: Cromme began his career at Saint Gobain and speaks excellent French. François Hollande has frequently received them both in private. Their views on competitivity are those of the ERT and, unsurprisingly, are opposed to those of labour and social movements. ERT doctrine is now also gospel at the top of the French Socialist and German centre right governments.[10]

As Peter Sutherland, a former EU commissioner, former WTO Director and ex-director of both British Petroleum and Goldman Sachs, has said, the ERT is 'more than a lobby group. Each member of ERT has access at the highest levels of government.' And indeed, the influence of these people and their cohesiveness is beyond the grasp of ordinary mortals – they breathe the rarefied air of true Davos Class paragons.

Naturally, TABD members all have multiple memberships in other business organizations, such as chambers of commerce or industry-wide groups. In Europe, the somewhat less Olympian haven for them is BusinessEurope (formerly called UNICE), until recently presided over by Baron Ernest-Antoine Seillière. It includes TNCs, but also smaller companies and claims '41 business federations in 35 countries'. BusinessEurope also contributes constantly to the official European agenda.

On the other side or the Atlantic, it's the same story.

Here the European–American Business Council (EABC) has been around since 1990, functioning as a kind of European Chamber of Commerce in Washington, DC and New York, wholly funded by its member companies. The Americans have their national counterpart organizations, such as the venerable National Association of Manufacturers or the American Business Council, not to mention the powerful United States Chamber of Commerce (USCC), without doubt the top lobbying organization in the world. In 2012 it spent $136 million, more than three times as much as the next biggest lobby group registered with the US Congress.[11] Usually the USCC concentrates on supporting the Republican Party, pushing business-friendly laws through Congress or bringing numerous lawsuits to the Supreme Court where, in recent years, cases decided in its favour have achieved a 68 per cent success rate.

The USCC has become extremely active on international trade issues as well. In October 2012, it joined forces with BusinessEurope to publish a blueprint on 'Regulatory Cooperation in the EU–US Economic Agreement' (now officially known as the TTIP). They argued that ridding the two economies of 'even half of these [regulatory] divergences' would lead to GDP increases of over $200 billion a year on both sides of the Atlantic. Their study on regulatory convergence includes a long description and checklist of what to do and how to do it and outlines the machinery needed to make US–EU rules entirely harmonious. This machinery, according to the US Chamber of Commerce, must be permanent in order to conform to the 'evergreen', or ongoing, permanently amendable approach. Never again, in their scenario, would national parliaments be in charge of setting the regulatory rules on new products and processes.

On-the-ground monitoring of international issues, above all trade, is the role of the *American* (as opposed to US) Chamber of Commerce, familiarly known as AmCham, with its 115 member offices in foreign countries, including a particularly important one in Brussels. AmCham has 15 specialized committees and sponsors frequent TTIP conferences in the EU's member countries under the aegis of the local government. All this represents a good deal of firepower.

CORPORATIONS, ORGANIZATIONS, PROLIFERATIONS

The Transatlantic Business Dialogue was the earliest and principal theatre for preparing the TTIP, but since it was founded in 1995, some confusing mutations have taken place. As of 1 January 2013, a newcomer, the Transatlantic Business *Council*, has emerged as the result of a merger between the TABD and the above-mentioned EABC. The TABD will continue to function as a distinct programme within this new council. Since 2007, we've also been blessed with yet another council – the Transatlantic *Economic* Council (TEC), set up by Chancellor Merkel, President Bush and EU Commission President Barroso. Is this just one more 'mechanics group' for greasing US/EU commercial wheels? Yes, except that the TEC goes much further. The first thing it tells the visitor to its site is:

> The Transatlantic Economic Council is a political body to oversee and accelerate government-to-government cooperation with the aim of advancing economic integration between the European Union and the United States of America.

A '*political* body'? to '*oversee and accelerate* . . . economic *integration*'? The TEC describes its goal as ridding us of bothersome regulations in order to 'empower the private sector'. It sounds like the US Chamber of Commerce/BusinessEurope blueprint for governing made flesh. Who said citizens wanted 'economic integration' to 'empower the private sector'? Do you remember anyone voting for any of this? I don't.

But perhaps we're just feeling a bit dizzy from all the councils, chambers and acronyms. These shouldn't get in the way of understanding the main purpose: the TNCs have been practising 'hands across the sea' for a couple of decades, merging and cooperating with each other and with their governments, creating their own *permanent, political, policymaking* institutions with the help of elected politicians. Now they think they are entitled to the payoff.

Through their sundry, more-or-less public organizations and entities, the companies have never deviated from their course: reduce and eliminate regulations, push down standards, smooth the pathway for business, 'harmonize' or integrate trade rules and, ultimately, economies under their guidance. These proliferating organizations all want the same things, including official permission and protection for companies to make the rules in the service of higher profits. It's not a scoop that corporations have interests and fully intend to defend them, but it is new that they have decided that they, not legislators or designated government offices, should be free to replace, or nearly, agencies like the Environmental Protection Agency or one of the numerous EU regulatory bodies scattered around the European landscape from Dublin to Parma to Warsaw.[12]

The TTIP itself is, however, at least a semi-scoop because it had been waiting in the wings, in gestation for nearly 20 years, unremarked by nearly everyone while gaining more and more elevated official standing. As Hilary Clinton, former US Secretary of State, has said, underlining its geopolitical aspects, 'it is as much a strategic imperative as an economic one'. Now it is also revealed as a serious menace to citizens on both sides of the Atlantic and to democracy itself. At the end of 2013 the declared official ambition was to sign the TTIP within a year. As of this writing, signatures sometime in 2015 looked more realistic to its supporters. Let us hope that opposition can put it off until doomsday.

This agreement would cover not just a massive share of world GDP and trade, but also the world's largest stock of investments. By 2012, their cumulative stock amounted to €2.8 trillion ($3.7 trillion) on one side or the other of the Atlantic, making the US–EU commercial relationship certainly the most substantial in the world.[13]

'More' here does not mean 'better', and if the TTIP is allowed to take privatization and deregulation further, it will very likely have a negative impact on citizens' lives, while enhancing TNC profits. As far as we know, and if it conforms to the WTO model, it will not contain a word concerning the protection of consumers and public health; no social provisions concerning work and workers; no binding rules to conserve nature or improve the environment.

DECODING: SO WHAT EXACTLY *IS* THE TTIP ABOUT?

Decoding the treaty can be more quickly accomplished than one might fear, given that most of it remains secret, in particular the potentially most dangerous chapters and articles. Sometimes the TNCs are secretive; sometimes shameless and occasionally both at once. The TTIP and its processes are outstanding examples of what they hope to hide, but fortunately we still have numerous clues to what they want. They clearly believe they can kill an entire flock of birds with the single stone marked Transatlantic Trade and Investment Partnership.

As we've seen, the TNCs have already obtained not just the consent, but also the enthusiastic cooperation of their governments. On a state visit to Washington in early 2014, François Hollande announced at a joint press conference with President Obama that they needed to 'accelerate' the TTIP negotiations in order to avoid the 'accumulation of fears, of threats, of tensions'. Up until then, the French government had not articulated this position and it is not clear exactly who or what Hollande thought was behind those 'threats'.[14]

Both the corporations and the governments seem to see the 'consent of the governed' as a quaint eighteenth-century constitutional notion. They are consequently convinced that their years of careful preparations, their confusing web of official and non-official organizations plus the opacity and complexity of the agreement itself guarantee that they can push it through without interference from the public.

In this, they are mistaken. The opposition is growing fast and is not without weapons for the battle against the TTIP. The sharpest of these is knowledge of the content – even if we have no access to the texts. One of the reliable sources we can use is the mandate from the European Council (i.e., the decision-making organ of the EU member states) whose secretariat asked members to authorize opening the negotiations. The members duly signed up, but the Commission had prepared the whole show and the mandating process was just a game of pass-the-parcel. The text shows that most of the details in the mandate had clearly been settled beforehand between the Commission, the governments and the corporations.[15] Member states had little to do with it and citizens nothing at all.

CONTENT PROVIDERS

Purported to be based on reports by a High Level Working Group (HLWG), the mandate is in fact a wish list from the corporate sector distributed via the unfailingly neoliberal Commission. Who participated in this HLWG that prepared the mandate? Don't ask. I did, through the service Europe Direct, which does its best to make European affairs transparent for European citizens. Europe Direct had no ready answer to my question, but helpfully sent it on to the Directorate General for

Trade, which eventually replied that 'there is unfortunately not a list of members of the High Level Working Group . . .'.

Chaired by the top negotiators on both sides of the Atlantic (which we knew anyway from the internet) the HLWG's reports, according to DG Trade, are the result of 'a common effort of various European Commission services . . . and the gathering of input provided by other Commission services, civil society and stakeholders', the whole affair coordinated by Directorate E of DG Trade.[16]

Who those 'civil society' input providers might be remains mysterious, but I can say for sure that they aren't any of the 55 European civil society organizations I know of that are worried about the TTIP and belong to the Alternative Trade Mandate group.[17] In EU-speak, 'civil society' generally means 'business' and you are only a 'stakeholder' if the Commission says you are. We can be quite sure that the HLWG complies with the 'of, by and for business' pattern.

This is confirmed by the diligence of Corporate Europe Observatory (CEO), which from April 2013 doggedly pushed the EU information services to supply documents concerning the Commission's preparations prior to launching the TTIP. CEO didn't get the full complement of documents they had asked for, but some results finally came trickling back in September, showing that of 127 listed meetings between January 2012 and April 2013, 119 – or 93 per cent – had taken place with large corporations and their lobbyists.

The records were heavily censored, but still showed that BusinessEurope and the automobile industry umbrella lobbying group ACEA enjoyed nine meetings each; other frequent guests were 'the US Chamber of Commerce, Digital Europe, the European Services Forum, and the Transatlantic Business Council' – and 'also numerous meetings with the arms industry, banking, medical technology, food, pharmaceutical and chemical lobbies'.[18]

OPPOSITION RISES, THE COMMISSION RETALIATES

Towards the end of 2013, the Commission, particularly DG Trade, clearly became somewhat panicked in face of the suddenly mounting opposition to its plans, and duly decreed a full-dress communications operation to sell TTIP to the public on the basis of 'Jobs and Growth'. In another leaked document, DG Trade rang the bells, calling all hands on deck to devote themselves to the 'management of stakeholders, social media and transparency'.[19] It's doubtless a good thing that ordinary citizens are not listed because if we qualified as 'stakeholders' we might resent being 'managed'.

They badly needed a public relations offensive, because the more that people understood about the TTIP, the less they liked it. The part of the HLWG report they always quote explains the marvellous benefits to be expected by the citizens of Europe and the USA:

> [T]he EU's economy could benefit by €119 billion a year – equivalent to an extra €545 for a family of four in the EU ... the US economy could gain an extra €95 billion a year or €655 per American family ... The TTIP would be the cheapest stimulus package imaginable.[20]

The Commission quotes these figures every chance it gets, but doesn't do the arithmetic to tell you what they actually mean. The GDP gain would amount to less than 1 per cent for the whole of Europe and the individual gain if evenly shared would be €2.60 a week.[21] The Commission also doesn't mention that even the think-tank authors, clearly in sympathy with the Commission's own purposes, admit these benefits would only come to pass by 2027 and that the gains per family promised are according to its own most 'ambitious and comprehensive' scenario. Other, less optimistic scenarios are never alluded to.

Now let's start decoding this political and economic scam with the title itself. The media that bother to report on it at all refer to the TTIP as a 'free trade agreement'. It would be more accurate to call it a Charter of TNC freedoms; a catalogue of rights unencumbered by any responsibilities.

First off, it's *not* called the TAFTA – Transatlantic Free Trade Agreement – as the Americans initially thought they should call it. Cooler heads prevailed: it had dawned on them that this rhyming title could rekindle painful memories of the NAFTA or North American Free Trade Agreement which over the past two decades has caused enormous losses of employment, land and livelihood for millions of workers, farmers and other citizens of North America and Mexico.

The harm done is worth brief elaboration since the TTIP promoters are making exactly the same claims as NAFTA-touting flunkies did before that agreement was passed in 1994. They promised a magic formula that could invigorate both the US and Mexican economies. The opposite happened, and disaster for ordinary people ensued. US-subsidized corn poured into Mexico and two million small farmers were forced off the land, unable to compete with the cheap imports. Thousands more were reduced to dire poverty. The price of the basic tortilla later went up by 50 per cent. The entry of huge retailers like Walmart, selling goods made by the world's cheapest labour in China and elsewhere, managed to ruin an estimated 28,000 small businesses in Mexico.

Now the USA is fighting the influx of Mexican immigrants, building walls and increasing border patrols. Meanwhile, since 1995, many thousands of desperate Mexicans attempting to cross the border have died from heat shock, drowning, accidents or vigilante murders. If one wants to curb immigration, the most effective policy would be to enhance people's chances to live and make good in the country where they were born, but this has apparently not occurred to the USA, nor for that matter to the EU, whose politicians think you can have it both ways.

The Economic Policy Institute in Washington, DC estimates Americans' job losses due to NAFTA at precisely 682,900.[22] Many US companies moved south of the border in order to use cheaper labour, but also to squash attempts to form trade unions. By the early 2000s, hundreds of these plants had moved again, this time to China – even though Mexican wages had already fallen quite drastically. Let us not forget that wages in Eastern Europe are in some cases 10 per cent of what skilled American workers can earn, but also that American wages are far below what many Europeans are paid.

Were these impacts a fluke? Perhaps so. But since NAFTA, the loss of well-paid manufacturing jobs has continued and 60,000 plants have closed down. This is not entirely due to free trade agreements, but globalization in general has played a large role. Furthermore, 'Barack Obama promised that the US–Korea Free Trade Agreement would increase US exports by $10 billion. They immediately fell by $3.5 billion. The 70,000 jobs it would deliver? Er, 40,000 were lost.'[23] So they didn't call their treaty the TAFTA, but chose Transatlantic Trade and Investment Partnership instead.

What does this name conceal? It is 'Transatlantic' – for sure, its aim is to bind the United States and the European Union together in a single set of rules. As we've seen, some zealots are already talking about US–EU 'integration'. And 'Trade'? Yes, again fair enough, it's about trade but not necessarily as most people would define the word. EU–US trade is already 'free' to a remarkable degree, with average tariffs at an almost insignificant 2 or 3 per cent. It would hardly be worth all the fuss just to reduce tariffs from their current levels.

RESOLUTION OF DISPUTES, DISSOLUTION OF DEMOCRACY

So is the treaty about an *investment* partnership? Yes, definitely. And central to all of the hundreds of bilateral or multilateral trade and investment treaties today is the dreaded ISDS, the Investor to State Dispute Settlement clause, which gives corporations the right to sue sovereign governments if a company can claim that a government measure will harm its present, or even its 'expected', future profits.

Those who remember the battle against the Multilateral Agreement on Investment (MAI) at the end of the 1990s will recall that the ISDS clause was the final outrage that caused that agreement to collapse. When people first heard about it, they were incredulous and understood instantly that this kind of 'justice' was a threat to democracy. ISDS gives transnational corporations the right to take their case before a private ad hoc arbitration tribunal if they considered they were being 'partially expropriated', or not being given 'fair and equitable treatment', standard elastic treaty phrases that can mean one thing today and seven different things tomorrow.

Campaigners against the MAI soon discovered that the ISDS was the best single tool in the activist kit for practising the 'Dracula Strategy': expose the vampire to the light of day and he will shrivel and die.

And shrivel he did, but he didn't die. When the MAI was defeated, the vampire just returned temporarily to his coffin and closed the lid. The TNCs never gave up on obtaining ISDS; indeed, they never give up on anything and from their point of view, they're right not to. Using NAFTA as the precedent, they soon got investor-to-state clauses inserted into innumerable treaties with more limited geographical scope and have since used the procedure to great advantage. At last count, in 2013 a cumulative 560-some cases had been registered in one or another arbitration forum and 244 decided. The number of cases initiated yearly is on the upswing: in 2012, 52 new complaints were brought, 60 per cent of which were initiated by European companies.

The highest compensation award ever decreed by an arbitration tribunal occurred in 2012 when Occidental Petroleum sued Ecuador for breach of contract. The tribunal found the government guilty and told Ecuador to pay compensation of $1.77 billion. Ecuador argued it was simply trying to prevent the company from drilling in a protected ecological reserve area, but that argument did not convince the arbitrators.[24]

The number of cases registered and decided given here is probably underestimated, because there is no central registry for ISDS disputes. Everything else about them is secret as well; no proceedings are held in public and no third parties such as environmental or labour activists are admitted.[25] Once decided, the verdict stands. No appeals are allowed.

A WINDFALL FOR LAWYERS

Lawyers are already rubbing their hands at the shower of gold they expect if the TTIP passes. At one festive evening of American law firms with branches in Brussels,

> attendees nibbled on foie gras lollipops, dipped in a chocolate fondant [as they] discussed the potential business bonanza from trans-Atlantic trade negotiations that recently began between Europe and the United States. The *goal of the negotiations is to 'harmonize' the regulatory systems of the United States and Europe*, so that companies can meet a single standard – worth hundreds of millions of dollars, if not billions, in savings for businesses, particularly if they can persuade negotiators to *accept less strict rules* in the process.[26] (my italics)

ISDS is just that, Investor to State but not 'SIDS' or State to Investor. There is no reciprocity – that is, governments cannot sue foreign corporations for damages if, for example, they cause harm to the environment, public health, public security, public property or otherwise don't respect their contract.[27] A government can't 'win'; it can only not lose. Foreign investors will be allowed to sue governments for measures claimed to harm their profits, present or future, whereas local investors will generally have no such right.

As one honest European professional arbitrator wrote:

> When I wake up at night and think about arbitration, it never ceases to amaze me that sovereign states have agreed to investment arbitration at all ... Three private individuals are entrusted with the power to review, without any restriction or appeal procedure, all actions of the government, all decisions of the courts, and all laws and regulations emanating from parliament.[28]

Arguments may well exist for hearing investment disputes before private arbitration tribunals in places where courts are notoriously corrupt and a fair trial would be impossible, but this cannot be said to be the case for Europe or for the United States.

The arbitrators and the lawyers work in a highly specialized branch of the legal profession and mostly come from top British and American firms, although thanks to the number of cases launched via proliferation of BITs, university courses in arbitration have also become available and professionals from other countries are joining the ranks. Nonetheless, according to Cecilia Olivet and Pia Eberhardt, it's still a small, tight club. Only 15 arbitrators had decided 55 per cent of the hundreds of cases they studied; the lawyers routinely charge an average $1,000 an hour for each of several in a team, and arbitrators get $3,000 a day.[29]

Governments, if they lose, also pay the costs, which so far have averaged about $8 million and in at least one case exceeded $30 million. Lawyers sometimes act as arbitrators. Cases can take a long time to be argued and decided – one resulted in an arbitrator earning close to a million dollars for a single case. When acting as arbitrators, they are paid case by case and thus have an incentive to counsel corporate clients to sue when they see the possibility of a handsome settlement. The arbitrator may also have an interest in ruling in favour of the corporate sector rather than the state in order to gain a repu-tation for 'generosity' to the complainant. When more awards lead to more clients, in plain language the financial stakes repre-sent a conflict of interest, and here it would seem to be innate to the process (although the arbitrators must be accepted by both sides).

The increasing number of complaints brought every year may reflect this situation. Genuine neutrality could be an extremely difficult frame of mind to attain and sustain. Nobody's per-fect, lawyers are human and can be subject to more-or-less unconscious motivations and biases. According to Olivet and Eberhardt:

> Arbitrators tend to defend private investor rights above public interest, revealing an inherent pro-corporate bias. Several prominent arbitrators have been members of the board of major multinational corporations ... [and] share businesses' belief in the paramount importance of protecting private profits ... Law firms with specialised arbitration departments seek out every opportunity to sue countries – encouraging lawsuits against governments in crisis, most recently Greece and Libya ... [and] encourage corporations to use lawsuit threats as a political weapon in order to weaken or prevent laws on public health or environmental protection.[30]

WHERE WILL DISPUTES ARISE?
SOME CONCRETE POSSIBILITIES

First, let me say that, despite this barrage of criticism, I'm not against free trade per se if it is also fair and if the weaker partners to an agreement are fully aware of what they are signing. I furthermore agree that duplicate, outdated and red-tape-ridden rules and regulations are bound to exist on one side, the other or both, and could easily be eliminated. Why go through the same tests twice if the competent government agencies are convinced that the regulations really *are* duplicates?

But how can we know if they are, especially when they are arrived at using different methodologies? I certainly wouldn't trust a bunch of TNCs to determine standards, whatever their national origin, particularly since we know that their political backers are themselves governing largely on behalf of the corporations and consult them constantly.

Nor would I necessarily trust all government agencies charged with setting and enforcing those standards – bureaucracies have interests too, and turf to protect. Again, it depends on the methodology and the interpretations. Since we are going to look briefly at the various areas where disputes and ISDS lawsuits are most likely to arise, we can start with the automobile industry to illustrate this point.

The USA, like the EU, obviously has standards for automobile safety and also has an executing agency, the National Highway Traffic Safety Administration (NHTSA). Some may recall the book called *Unsafe at Any Speed* that first made Ralph Nader famous. Published in 1965, it was full of alarming news about the dire inadequacy of US standards and told the story of the car manufacturers' aversion to spending any money at all on safety features, including seatbelts. Have those days passed? You be the judge.

Almost 50 years later, General Motors (which had to be

saved from bankruptcy by US taxpayers in 2008) was finally ordered to recall six of its models – 2.6 million cars in all worldwide – whose ignition can simply switch off without warning, as has happened when drivers were in the middle of an intersection or driving at high speed on freeways. Thirteen deaths have been positively attributed to this dangerous defect, although that is GM's own figure and only a percentage of the total. The toll has to be higher because unnumbered deaths and injuries are not taken into account. From February 2003, the regulatory agency admits to receiving an average of two complaints a month about engine shutdowns and their human – not to mention financial – consequences, but did nothing because 'there was not enough evidence'. We only know about this because a team of *New York Times* reporters themselves sifted through the complaints that the NHTSA found insufficient to act upon – whereas the complaints had continued to pile up for 11 years. The question is not the presence or the absence of standards, but their quality and above all their enforcement.[31]

A great deal is wrong with Europe but, in general, European standards for health, safety, security and the environment are higher and more stringent than those of the United States.

Beyond specific differences related to each regulatory area, the basic philosophies that underlie the two systems also diverge markedly. The US model consists in setting standards and then, should they prove insufficient or too lenient, to provide for changes through complaints and litigation. Consumers or others who consider themselves wronged by a company or harmed by a product can bring 'class action' lawsuits and try to obtain justice and compensation from the corporation after the fact. These court judgments will then presumably lead to stricter rules.

In Europe, the 'precautionary principle' is much more frequently invoked: when in doubt, do not allow. This principle underpins the European refusal to import hormone-fed beef and, to a lesser degree, the banning of some – though certainly not all – genetically modified crops. No single definition of the precautionary principle – or PP – exists, but the one used in the Rio Declaration on Environment and Development in 1992 can be applied to many other areas:

> In order to protect the environment, the precautionary approach shall be widely applied by states according to their capabilities. Where there are threats of serious or irreversible damage, lack of full scientific certainty shall not be used as a reason for postponing cost-effective measures to prevent environmental degradation.[32]

Such precautions are especially needed in health matters since, for the foreseeable future, it will remain virtually impossible to relate chemical or substance X to illness or outcome Y. Science could handle the question of, say, asbestos, because it causes a relatively rare cancer in specific populations that worked with, or lived with, asbestos, but such direct links are rare. A responsible doctor will warn you that if you are taking five or more different medicines regularly, there are bound to be unpredictable interactions.

However, the United States demands irrefutable proof and US industry never speaks of the PP without calling it 'the so-called precautionary principle'. It refuses the argument that absolute certainty, particularly where the human body is concerned, is scientifically impossible, at least at our present stage of scientific advancement. What US critics of the PP – and they are legion – call 'sound science' does not mean identifying the presence or absence of a high degree of risk, but being 100 per cent proof positive.

What are the chances that people will be able to judge if the European bureaucracy is willing to change, eliminate or 'harmonize' certain standards in order to conform to the text of a 'trade' agreement? The answer to that is simple – there's no chance at all. The public won't know what's on the table in the first place. Let us recall the obstacles of secrecy and opacity: I cannot, and no layperson without an entry ticket to the corporate universe can, swear that standards will be lowered or concessions made on a given subject by one side or the other and we are not likely to learn the details until the show is over. So we can only look at the probabilities of where attacks will be directed and against which standards.[33]

Even in the European Parliament, only a few MEPs on the trade committee are allowed – not actually to see the texts, heaven forbid – but to attend briefings by Trade Commissioner Karel de Gucht, exclusively in English with no interpreters present, during which de Gucht tells them as much or as little as he chooses about the ongoing talks. For those of us who do not see the Commission's pronouncements as second only to the Ten Commandments in truth and authority, here are a few details on areas where deregulation could well occur and are therefore worth watching.[34]

Food and agriculture

These vital sectors will probably be harder hit by TTIP than any others in Europe and, as happened in Mexico with NAFTA, small farmers are likely to be the biggest losers. Specialty farms might survive, but most cereals and oilseeds producers won't. Although the family farm sector in Europe is shrinking drastically, and some EU politicians seem to want to wipe it out entirely, we still have 13.7 million farms; in the USA only 2.2 million remain, many of them far larger than even the biggest ones in Europe.[35]

European tariffs are also a lot higher than American ones, largely to prevent the entry of heavily subsidized US produce. Smaller European farmers are already up against the Common

Agricultural Policy (CAP), which gives far more advantages to large farms. The highest farmer suicide rates in the world are in India and France. Free-traders everywhere would immediately say, 'fine, cut the tariffs and see who wins'. We know the answer already: subsidized crops would win because the subsidies would be disguised, huge American feedlots for beef cattle would win against small-scale European farmers whose animals are mostly pastured. Economies of scale with lower standards would win.

Free-traders would win, although they do not ask, nor answer, such rude questions as those concerning food sovereignty – who produces what, for whom, according to whose standards; whether Europeans want to eat beef laced with hormones and antibiotics; if they accept GMO cereals and unlabelled GMO products; fruits treated with pesticides outlawed in Europe or raw chickens washed with chlorine. They don't ask where ruined and displaced farmers would go or who would employ them. They aren't interested in who would take care of the countryside or the 'rural deserts' that would inevitably follow the abandoning of the European small farming sector. Nor do they worry about where our future food might come from in case of massive droughts or floods; what our consumers could tolerate in case of severe shortages and price increases; and what, if any, control we might have over any of these factors. The TTIP is an anti-food sovereignty charter.

The US agricultural industries know precisely what they want:

> [an] ambitious ... chapter based on science and international standards ... [and an end to] unjustifiable restrictions on production methods that negatively affect exports of US meat, poultry, and fresh fruits; costly and ever changing political and regulatory barriers to agricultural biotechnology that restrict US corn, soy and processed corn and soy product exports;

and imposition of arbitrary sustainability requirements . . . Such unscientific measures have become the most challenging barrier to US food and agricultural exports to the EU.[36]

The letter to the US chief TTIP negotiator, from which this quote is taken, is signed by 64 US transnational agricultural corporations, producers' federations and associations representing just about every conceivable crop, meat product or specialty, including the Seed Trade Association and US Livestock Genetics Export, Inc.

The US side is also against any compulsory food labelling, including disclosure of GMOs in food products – the food processing industry sees labelling as an unnecessary cost. This huge industry coalition also wants its negotiators to attack European 'geographical indications' (GIs) – the kind of product protection that says that 'champagne' comes from the Champagne region of France – not California or Australia. Lots of European cheeses, wines and other foodstuffs fit this category, but US producers maintain that 'products that have been in common use around the world for many years' should not be allowed to hide behind GIs 'and other such protectionist measures'. They give no examples. Don't consumers also want to know the provenance of what they eat?

The subject of GMOs makes the Americans positively bristle. They treat GMO food exactly like any other, whereas Europeans limit approvals of GMO crops and require labelling. A practical man, Andreas Geiger, who happens also to be managing partner of a leading EU lobbying law firm, has an idea:

[Recognizing the opportunity presented by the fact that] US farmers have been frustrated by these barriers for years, the US government is pushing towards concessions by the EU in this area ... and the US Senate Finance Committee has recently stressed that any agreement must also reduce EU

restrictions . . . reaching consensus on this issue is vital to successful negotiations of the TTIP.

Geiger concludes that the best solution for the US food industry giants is to stop expecting results through government
pressures and diplomacy, and instead – what else – 'engage in
hard-core lobbying activity themselves'. European firms use US
lobbyists in Washington and US agribusiness should follow suit:

> seek professional lobbying services on the TTIP issue . . . rely
> on firms that understand sensitivities in Europe [and] will come
> up with the most convincing arguments. [They] have the best
> chance to change Brussels' stance on GMOs now.[37]

Great! Not just progress on the TTIP and the billions it promises, but more business for law and lobbying firms like Geiger's
own.

Whether it's Europeans' refusal of hormone-fed beef,
chlorine-bathed chickens or GMOs, the US response is unfailingly that it's irrational, not 'scientific' or 'non-science based'.

Chemicals

European environmental activists find the EU chemicals directive
REACH (Registration, Evaluation, Authorization and Restriction
of Chemicals) too lenient and say it's being implemented far too
slowly, but it is still much better than the standards accepted
in the United States, where many chemicals banned outright
in Europe are freely in use. In the USA it can take as long as
20 years to get a single substance banned. As scientific studies
advance, dangerous new products have to be added to the list
and new battles fought all the time, for example on endocrine
or hormonal systems disruptors.

Tens of thousands of chemicals, present in foods and ordinary household products, are potential disruptors which can – at certain doses – lead to cancers, birth defects, cognitive and brain disorders in children and many other ill effects that occur during pregnancy. Do we want an American system, which will test the compounds one by one, with the chemical industry fighting change every step of the way, or outright bans on entire classes of chemicals known to increase risks?

Once more, we're up against two diverging philosophies on the two sides of the ocean. The Americans authorize a chemical that has not been irrefutably proven harmful; the Europeans – at least when pushed by public opinion – tend to use the precautionary principle. And if the companies can continue to produce and sell the same old and probably dangerous compounds, why should they bother to do research on newer and safer ones?

The EU has a lot to answer for as well. One of the Commission's purposes in pushing the TTIP in the EU is to 'harmonize' rules between member states so that no EU country could adopt *stronger* rules as, for example, the French did when they banned bisphenol A – an endocrine disruptor used in food product wrappings.[38] The European chemical industry is also trying to ram through legislation that would end the precautionary approach to agricultural and household chemicals.[39]

Fracking and shale gas

Hydraulic fracturation, better known as fracking, to extract gas from rock formations is also likely to become a hot subject for Investor to State disputes. Under the NAFTA ISDS clause, a US corporation called Lone Pine Resources is suing the Canadian province of Quebec for $250 million. Quebec's 'crime' is to have placed a moratorium on fracking – in other words, it took a legal initiative in view of the damage it considered fracking was doing. Lone Pine's lawsuit claims that Quebec's action was 'arbitrary, capricious and illegal' and caused the company the

'loss of a valuable right . . . without due process, without compensation and with no cognizable public purpose'. Lone Pine
claimed it also had a right to expect 'a stable economic and legal
environment'.[40]

One could point out that a 'stable legal environment' could
perfectly well be taken to mean 'no new laws at all' no matter
what new circumstances may come to light. A single example:
official research carried out by the Pennsylvania Department
of Environmental Protection shows dangerous increases in
levels of barium and strontium in ground water close to fracking sites, as well as an alarming variety of hazardous chemicals
such as arsenic, chloride and radium. Wells notoriously leak
and the storage of wastewater from the drilling is haphazard
and also leaks. Some of the wastewater, according to a Duke
University study, is dumped directly into water sources for
major Pennsylvania cities like Pittsburgh. The Pennsylvania
Department of the Environment has little capacity to regulate
and nowhere near the personnel to monitor thousands of fracking wells that have made the state the third largest source of
natural (shale) gas in the USA.[41]

The US fracking story gets even more problematic. In 2005,
under the presidency of George W. Bush, the whole US fracking industry got an exemption under the Safe Drinking Water
Act. Dean Baker, co-Director of the Center for Economic
Policy Research in Washington, DC alerts us to another danger
American citizens could face from both US and European companies under TTIP. European energy corporations might well
want to invest in fracking in the USA, where the industry has
much greater freedom than in Europe. Because the US government gave all shale gas-drillers

> a special exemption from laws on clean drinking water . . . they
> don't even have to disclose the chemicals they are using in
> the fracking process. As a result, if they end up contaminating

drinking water in areas near a fracking site, it will be almost impossible for victims to prove their case.[42]

Indeed, lawyers would have an easy time arguing that the names and properties of those chemicals are 'proprietary information' and therefore the drillers that use them are under no obligation to disclose them. They could also argue that the contamination didn't come from fracking at all but from previous activities in Pennsylvania, which is after all an industrial state – one with a long history of mining and drilling for oil and gas which they could claim were the real culprits. The damage caused to water supplies and the environment could be incalculable and in this industry, corporations would be particularly likely to win their lawsuits.

Intellectual property and Big Pharma

They would win because proprietary information is another weapon in the TTIP arsenal. Baker is also extremely worried about the damage US demands under the treaty could do to European citizens' health and to their governments' health-care systems. His fear is grounded in the intellectual property rules and patent protections the Americans will be fighting for through the TTIP.[43]

The US population spends nearly $350 billion a year on pharmaceuticals. The difference between the price to the consumer and the costs of production are so vast that drugs in the United States 'would sell for around one-tenth this price in a free market'. The TTIP is not concerned with establishing a 'free market', but with protecting 'proprietary information'. Oligopolies and the corporations want to prevent far cheaper, identical generic drugs from entering the market. Europeans now pay only about half what Americans do for drugs, so the companies' aim is to make patents stronger and last longer.

Patents are now granted for a 20-year period, but few truly new and important drugs have been invented in the past 20 years – leaving doors open, under present circumstances, to generics.

This is also a big issue in the TTP (Transpacific) agreement involving countries where millions of poor people would have zero access to medicines if they had to pay prices similar to those in the USA. In the United States itself, the government flagship anti-HIV/AIDS programme relies for 98 per cent of its drugs on generics. The pharmaceutical industry wants a legal system that allows them to 'evergreen' their patents – meaning make tiny changes which can prolong the life of their ownership indefinitely. Generic drugs everywhere could be wiped out and Big Pharma could charge whatever it wanted for its products.

We could tell a story about just about any other human activity that could lead to trade and therefore trade disputes between US and European companies and US and European governments. All new environmental regulation – such as emissions laws and ceilings on CO_2 – would be at high risk, because climate change is being constantly reconfirmed by ever more alarming scientific studies. Despite all the lobbying force of the largest CO_2 emitters, governments might decide that they finally had to act. The oil, gas and coal industries have very deep pockets and could sustain any number of lawsuits – and they are also financially far more powerful than a good many EU member states. Which path would they choose if governments tried to force them to reduce their emissions?

Government procurement at all levels would have to be opened to bids from all the TTIP countries and it would be impossible to reserve any public works for local or national companies. No restrictions on investment, such as requiring local content or local employment, could be enforced. Such would be the case at every level of government, from municipal to national to European Union. Labour codes and laws would be under heavy pressure. The French company Veolia is suing Egypt under ISDS because it passed a law to increase the minimum wage. Financial industry regulations would also be 'harmonized' and we know how powerful the banking lobbies are. In this sector, the Americans are a little better than the Europeans, but all would be hostile to taxes on financial transactions or to an effective separation of commercial (retail) and investment banks. Privacy and the internet would be at risk and free content could be threatened.

Lori Wallach is a redoubtable American lawyer who heads the trade department at the US NGO Public Citizen and has waged great campaigns against the MAI and other free trade agreements. She points out that countries don't need to sign up for clear infringements of national sovereignty like the ISDS to obtain investment. Brazil has signed no bilateral investment treaties at all and is the largest target of foreign investment in Latin America. But don't expect companies not to sue if they see a chance to prevent new laws or strike down old ones – everything in the TTIP is about obtaining the maximum of special privileges for corporations at the expense of democratic government.

THE EU COUNTER-OFFENSIVE

When by late 2013 people were beginning to entertain serious doubts about the TTIP, the Trade Directorate's communications charm offensive invented a Q&A sheet full of sweetness and light. Don't worry about anything and, by the way, anything you might be reading right now by the present author or others like her is nothing but a tissue of lies. We can assure you that nothing you might fear from TTIP is a cause for concern. Here is a sampling of the questions (italics in the 'answers' are mine), followed by remarks:[44]

Do I have to worry about existing EU standards of consumer, environment or health protection?

No. We will not negotiate existing levels of protection for the sake of an agreement. Our high level of protection here in Europe is *non-negotiable* ... [T]he US also takes protection of its citizens very seriously ... but we go about it in different ways ... There is room to learn from each other. There will be *no compromise whatsoever* on safety, consumer protection or the environment.

I'm sure we are all relieved to hear this. The problem is that in this Q&A, the Trade Directorate isn't actually talking about negotiations with a savvy and determined superpower, but rather writing a letter to Santa Claus. US transnational corporations have been quite frank about their contempt for the precautionary principle and declared clearly what they expect to get out of the treaty.[45]

Are we to believe as well that the European Union itself has no 'offensive' interests? Nothing it wants to obtain for itself? Or worse, that the Commission has no hidden desires to get rid of a lot of rules that constrain its own TNCs and would happily see them abolished? Unfortunately for the communications people, European citizens are not fools – they know that in any negotiation, particularly one prepared for years and constantly overseen by the corporate sector, you do not get everything you want and certainly not everything you only pretend to want. Hypocrisy can always be explained away: 'We did everything we could to get X but the other side was adamant.'

As Shaun Donnelly, formerly a US trade official, now a lobbyist for the US Council for International Business, puts it, 'TTIP is only worth doing if the regulatory side is covered, such as getting rid of the precautionary principle'.[46] Something's got to give, meaning in this case that Europe will have to give away a good many democratically arrived-at regulations, particularly because it's the main concern of the opposite side.

It's also the main concern of the most influential 'stakeholders' on the European side. Take it from Markus Beyrer of BusinessEurope: 'Regulatory differences must be eliminated. And not just the existing ones. We must prevent new ones from emerging.' Something will indeed have to give – this would be true even if the EU negotiators were free of all corporate influence, which they demonstrably are not.

At best, the most optimistic interpretation of the Q&A statement 'we will not negotiate *existing* levels of protection', could be understood as 'but we won't improve them either', since any improved standards will open the door to an EU member state being attacked with an ISDS lawsuit. And, as we'll see in the following chapter, they might also move the most controversial regulatory questions to a special vehicle.

Will European supermarkets be filled with meat from American animals fed with hormones?
No, they will not. The negotiations will not be about compromising the health of our consumers for commercial gain.

The mainstream European Consumer Association, which represents 40 different national consumer protection groups in Europe, is not so sure. Its director-general, Monique Goyens, says, 'We are not against TTIP as a consumer organization . . . [but] I would really not see the interest of US business in entering this agreement if there is not a lowering of some of the European standards.'[47]

Are the EU and US going to harmonise their standards?
No, *harmonisation is not on the agenda* . . . The TTIP is not about trying to convince each other to change our respective

systems, but rather about finding ways to make our systems work more smoothly.

How curious. I thought we heard those US lawyers say, via the *New York Times* and between nibbles on *foie gras* lollipops, that 'the goal of the negotiations is to "harmonize" the regulatory systems of the United States and Europe, so that companies can meet a single standard – worth hundreds of millions of dollars, if not billions, in savings for businesses." Someone has clearly misinformed the lawyers.

The EU Q&A also deals with the ISDS process and the arbitration tribunals:

> *Why is the EU including Investor to State Dispute Settlement in the TTIP?*
> The European Commission, the EU Member States and the European Parliament all believe that Investor to State Dispute Settlement (ISDS) is an important tool for protecting EU investors abroad. The fact that a country has *a strong legal system does not always guarantee foreign investors will be adequately protected.* ... Although the EU and the US are developed economies, investors can still come across problems affecting their investments which their domestic courts systems are not always able to deal with effectively.

These arguments concerning what the EU will or won't negotiate and the justifications for ISDS are curious, and in this case actually at odds with what other people in the Trade Directorate themselves say. In particular, the Directorate's spokesperson, Mr John Clancy, was more truthful than the Q&A about ISDS. He explained that

> The reason ISDS is needed in TTIP is that the US system does not allow companies to use international agreements like TTIP

as a legal basis in national courts. So European companies . . . will only be able to enforce the agreement through an international arbitration system like ISDS.[48]

How interesting. Well, now we know. The United States consistently refuses to recognize all kinds of international law, including the Vienna Convention on the Law of Treaties, which places these treaties above national law. It hasn't signed the Kyoto Protocol on climate change. It hasn't signed six out of eight basic conventions of the International Labour Organization or the UNESCO Convention on Cultural Diversity. It hasn't even signed the UN Convention on the Rights of the Child – and is now the only country in the world in that position, since the other hold-out, Somalia, ratified it in early 2015, the 195th state to do so.

So instead of accepting legitimate, public courts in Europe as the proper venue for trials if American TNCs want to sue – because the USA would then have to let European companies sue the US government in US courts – the United States insists on a private arbitration system for everybody, destined to grant corporations unwarranted rights – not to mention generating lucrative business for prestigious law firms and forcing taxpayers to cough up the sums necessary to pay the costs of the trials and the financial awards granted.

The EU obviously accepts this denial of sovereignty and affront to democratic institutions as A Good Thing. Otherwise it could have told the USA to go home and revisit its own law, after which we could talk about the TTIP again.

It's also curious that the Q&A should insist that 'The fact that a country has a strong legal system does not always guarantee foreign investors will be adequately protected.' Already, without any TTIP, literally trillions of dollars or euros have been invested by the US in the EU or vice-versa. We haven't heard a great and rising clamour from investors that States have deprived the corporations of protection and expertly mugged them. When the European Commission first brought a case against Microsoft for abuse of its dominant position, violation of competition law and ordered the company to pay a fine of nearly €500 million, Microsoft wasn't happy but eventually paid up. That, however, was nearly a decade ago.

CONCLUSION

Giving in without the slightest hesitation to corporate pressure and handing over judicial power to the private sector seem not to bother the Commission (nor, obviously, the US government). The EU member states and their taxpayers will have to pay the costs for the trials and compensation to the companies claiming losses because elected governments have got in the way of their profits. Regulation, if the EU gets its way and as we shall see in the following pages, will be entirely removed from the hands of citizens and their elected representatives. Either the Commission agrees that all this is perfectly fine and normal, or it is unwilling to contest the issue. EU member states – our own governments – must agree too, since they all signed the mandate which includes ISDS. What should we conclude? You can take your pick: either we are governed by the spineless and supine or by anti-democratic forces willingly corrupted by the TNCs, or, come to think of it, both.

The TTIP is a despotic and direct assault of the Davos Class oligarchy and its appointed political servants against democracy. We don't need the special exception for audiovisual products and services France is so proud of obtaining. Or if we do, then we also need the health exception, the labour rights exception, the pharmaceuticals, the environmental, the social, the financial, the regulations . . . exceptions until nothing remains to be discussed.

The only decent course of action is to get up from the table, close the door politely and leave an empty chair.

3

REGULATORY COOPERATION:
MORE DANGER AHEAD

All the wrangling over the Transatlantic Trade and Investment Partnership shows that the issues of standards, norms and regulations are crucial for business. Seen from Brussels, Washington and executive suites on both continents, they are not necessary protections for health, safety and the environment, but 'obstacles to trade'. When corporate spokespersons are being polite, they call them BBBs for Behind Borders Barriers or TBTs for Technical Barriers to Trade; when less polite, 'trade irritants' or '£$%^&*! unnecessary rules'.[1]

They try to justify their obsession with deregulation by claiming it will be good for everyone. Recall the TTIP sales pitch and the promises the Commission makes about increased incomes for 'European families' which are supposed to come, in future, largely from doing away with the regulations the companies claim are costing them billions. The assumption is that trade and thus economic growth will increase and that any savings for the corporations will be automatically passed on to consumers, not to shareholders and corporate brass.

They are free to say this just as you and I are to say they are exaggerating.

Statements by well-placed business people or negotiators confirm that, in their view, the TTIP isn't worth bothering with if it doesn't include across-the-board deregulation. At the same time, widespread knowledge and resistance to the treaty are growing and the issue is coming to resemble the old riddle of physics – 'What happens when an immovable object meets an irresistible force?' What happens when an adamant demand from business meets the force of public opinion?

This is another area in which governments prove their usefulness to the companies and it provides further evidence that TNCs cannot dispense with government. They need to work hand in hand with elected officials and unelected bureaucrats. Even when the corporations and the political leadership want the same things, neither can obtain them alone because the people can get in the way. Elected politicians could balk at supporting the TTIP if its contents became too well known and too many citizens stood firmly against the deregulation it promises. The unelected politicians (commissioners, US trade representatives, high-level ministry people) don't want to be seen as politicians, but as neutral technicians or as diplomats working for the common good. The companies don't want to be seen pulling the strings of their marionettes in Brussels or Washington, much less be visibly sitting at the negotiating table. In the case of the TTIP, as it becomes better known, it looks as if the best option for all could be *not to deregulate*.

What? Not go after the prize the TNCs claim is worth tens if not hundreds of billions to them? Exactly – despite adverse public opinion, they could still win out against citizen awareness by engineering a devious displacement of the regulatory provisions now in the treaty to some other legal instrument. Then they could announce that that there will be no deregulation under the TTIP. Note that they've already tried to claim just that in the Q&A Commission document we quoted at the end of the previous chapter. If they leave in all the regulatory issues now present in the TTIP, the Commission's exercises in public relations won't hold up to even casual scrutiny.[2]

But what if it were 'true' that the TTIP won't deregulate, in the sense that deregulation would indeed be removed from the body of the treaty itself and put somewhere else instead where citizens would have no say and parliament no veto power? Why wouldn't the Commission – which alone has the initiative to propose laws – choose such a stealth-bomber approach as it did, for example, in 2005 when popular referenda allowed the French and the Dutch to reject overwhelmingly the Constitutional Treaty?

When those results came in, the Commission was stunned, but it reacted fast, brought together a group of the faithful (names withheld from the public) and instructed them to draw up a new instrument. This was the Lisbon Treaty, under which we are living today. Except for a few symbolic items such as the Beethoven hymn and the flag which were thrown out, it mimicked almost exactly the defeated constitution, while making all the legal provisions even harder to access and to understand than they had been before. As the principal author of the text of the defeated constitution, Valéry Giscard d'Estaing said at the time, 'They have made cosmetic changes to make it easier to swallow.' The new-old treaty was then duly ratified, this time without allowing misguided and troublesome people in member states to vote on the matter.

Today, despite all their preparatory work, advances and advantages, it's now fair to say that both the TNCs and the Commission are worried enough to have developed a fall-back position in case there's a snag. They fear the TTIP could turn into something like a repeat performance of the MAI – the Multilateral Agreement on Investment that collapsed in 1998

when citizen protests pushed the French government to withdraw and others followed.

What if governments once again concluded that the TTIP was
turning out to be too costly for them politically? What if they
told the Commission to get out of the way and refused to sign?
What if French President Hollande finally understood he was
destroying the Socialist Party and that signing the TTIP could be
the final nail in its coffin? Granted, that's a lot of ifs, but remember Dracula who cannot face the light of day. The more people
know, the more they resist and the deeper the stake is driven
into the vampire's heart.

The pro-TTIPers could choose a variety of strategies. They
might decide simply to identify the regulations that are truly
time- and resource-consuming duplicates on both sides of
the Atlantic; then declare that if the product or process has
passed the test on one side, there's no need to run it again on
the other. They might remove the subjects that have truly hit
the headlines and fired the public imagination and opposition –
GMOs, hydraulic fracking, hormone beef, chlorine chicken, and
the like – put them away for a rainy day and concentrate on
those regulations that may seem more abstract, such as labour
laws, CO_2 emissions, privatization of public enterprises and so
on. Some provisions could stay in the TTIP and some would be
put on the agenda of a new Regulatory Cooperation Council,
about which more in a moment. But they would find a way to
play it safe or at least more safely than it's being played now.
Naturally they are not going to make any public announcements
concerning which strategy they choose and ordinary citizens
can only speculate, as I am doing here. But they are bound to
want to please business and allow the TNCs to get their way by
whatever means, duplicity included.

The EU and US have a long history of discussing regulatory
matters and are far from starting from scratch. They began
exploring the subject in about 1990 as a part of the regular

EU–US summit meetings. The Transatlantic Business Dialogue did this sort of work from the time it was established in 1995; the Transatlantic Economic Partnership also had regulation on its agenda from 1998 and followed up with guidelines and a road-map for 'EU–US Regulatory Cooperation and Transparency'. Then came the Transatlantic Economic Council in 2007 and in 2011 the High Level Working Group – that shadowy deal-maker for which you can't obtain a list of the members. It's clear they're not about to give up. The HLWG was the latest body to give a high-level shove to making regulation central to US–EU relations as things heated up and they prepared to launch the TTIP.[3]

Now we'll hark back to the quite technical 2012 paper on 'Regulatory Cooperation in the EU–US Economic Agreement' mentioned in the previous chapter. The 'economic agreement' it refers to is now known as the TTIP and the US Chamber of Commerce and BusinessEurope drew it up six months before the treaty talks began. It's a quite explicit blueprint on how to deal with regulatory issues. Their stated goal was:

> [to ensure that] US and EU regulators determine where their regulatory regimes aim for compatible regulatory outcomes, such that *a product or service that can be sold in one market can be made available for purchase in the other;* and provide *new tools and a governing process* to guide regulatory cooperation on both a cross-cutting and sector-specific basis, which will help *address divergences in both the existing stock of regulations and in future regulatory measures*. . .creating an '*evergreen process* with a *continuous agenda* for advancement'.[4]

Let's translate this: The TNCs have never strayed from their course – recall also the forthright Transatlantic Business Dialogue slogan of 20 years ago: 'Approved Once, Accepted Everywhere.' Whatever is sold in one market can be sold in others, period. That's still what they want: We've approved it and the rest of you may go home now and keep quiet.

They are also saying: We, the two wealthiest and most powerful business lobbying organizations on either side of the Atlantic have joined forces to demand harmonization of rules both general and particular ('cross-cutting and sector-specific'); we want the agreement to be retroactive and cover all $3 trillion-worth of US–EU existing investments, plus future ones. This agreement must also provide for a permanent or 'ever-green' transatlantic jurisdictional institution. This body will be in charge of all EU–US regulation from now on, whether established in the past, the present or the future. It will determine the conditions under which anything that can be traded – goods, services, agricultural products, intellectual property, processes etc. – will be acceptable in both the EU and the US.

PLAYING CHICKEN? A TEST CASE

Common or 'harmonized' regulations being central to this business plan, let's test their concept against a concrete, nuts-and-bolts case of a likely future American regulation. Since 2011, the US Department of Agriculture has been asking legislators for a cost-cutting plan to regulate poultry slaughtering which the industry has been pushing for several years. The aim is twofold: (i) speed up the slaughtering line and (ii) make plant workers rather than government inspectors responsible for oversight and safety.

The current chicken-processing rule is 140 birds maximum per minute: it could go as high as 175, while reducing the number of inspectors by 75 per cent. 'In return, the government would require that processors bathe each chicken carcass in chlorine and other chemicals.' Don't ask me how it is humanly possible to deal under present regulations with 2.3 birds per second and still expect to increase that rate to nearly three:

that is what the news report says, but it isn't the point for the poultry industry or for the US Department of Agriculture.

Meanwhile, more than 100 American labour, consumer and public health groups have mobilized to protest, saying the employees would be endangered by the speed-up and made responsible for protecting consumers without receiving any training of the sort routinely provided for government inspectors. The protesters have been joined by groups representing minority, vulnerable and poor workers – poultry-slaughtering jobs are mostly filled by African American women. Their employers justify the changes, claiming that increasing 'processing speeds would save more than 250 million dollars a year'.[5]

So what will European regulators say? Will 28 EU member states refuse to import any US chickens on grounds of health, safety, consumer protection and human rights? Will they align their own regulations with those of the United States, saying OK to fowls bathed in chlorine and 'other chemicals' in, say, Brittany, where the French chicken-processing industry is based? Which other chemicals? We would be extremely lucky if anyone gave us or our elected representatives the chance to debate the matter, because with a hand-picked regulatory cooperation structure set up by business, rule-making is not going to be an open, transparent, accountable or democratic undertaking. Again, kindly return to your homes and keep quiet: we know what's best.

Now that the TTIP negotiations are in full swing, business interests on both sides of the Atlantic have been moving more aggressively on the subject. In the past, US companies have often complained bitterly on subjects such as GMOs, the REACH directive on chemicals and the precautionary principle in general, but now they are seizing the hormone-and-antibiotics-stuffed bull by the horns.

According to the *Financial Times*, US companies argue that the TTIP should be used to obtain 'fundamental change in the way business regulations are drafted in the EU'. They want access to EU decision-makers for American TNCs fully equivalent to that enjoyed by European corporations 'to allow [US] business groups greater input earlier in the process'. The Americans also 'complain that they are often shut out of the regulatory process in Europe . . . the EU system can depend on closed consultations with local industry groups that make it difficult for outsiders to register their concerns.'[6] Well, the TTIP is being touted as a huge job-creating machine, so why shouldn't lots of those jobs go to lobbyists for US corporate interests in Brussels?

Brussels, in the person of Commissioner de Gucht, replied to the US offensive that the EU would be willing to make some changes: 'We are ready to work in that direction but we cannot completely copy their [the US] system.'

Fair enough. But was de Gucht being entirely candid about his intentions? The poor man was on record as saying 'nothing under this agreement will lower standards of protection'. Note the carefully chosen words 'under this agreement'. He had to say something of the sort because any negotiation implies give-and-take and, by definition, neither side ever gets everything it wants. But what if lower standards were achieved under some *other* agreement? Then de Gucht would have been in the clear and not, at least not technically, lying.

RCC DOES NOT STAND FOR 'RENEWED CONCERN FOR CITIZENS'

In early December 2013 another leaked Commission document cast serious doubt on what official Europe is really up to. This EU *Position Paper* concerns the chapter on 'regulatory coherence' in the TTIP, and supplies its plans for shaping a new institution to deal with past, present and future regulation. The paper reads as though the matter has already been decided.

Perhaps it has – as usual, citizens have no access to the chapter concerned and will be the last to know.[7]

The paper announces that 'a Regulatory Cooperation Council (RCC) **will** be established'. It will meet regularly and include 'senior level representatives from regulators/competent authorities and trade representatives'. They will analyse 'joint submissions from EU and US stakeholders' on how to 'deepen regulatory cooperation towards increased compatibility for both future and existing regulatory measures'. The RCC will prepare a yearly regulatory programme and will be free to set up 'relevant' or 'ad hoc working groups'. It will interact with 'legislators (US Congress and the European Parliament)'. The '[precise or legal] relationship between the RCC and decision-making bodies under TTIP should be considered at a later stage'.[8]

Again, let's translate the various points the Commission makes on this future RCC which 'will' (not 'might', 'could' or 'should') be established. It will be permanent, dealing with past, present and future rules and regulations and therefore 'evergreen'. 'Stakeholders' (not ordinary citizens unless the RCC says so) will be invited to cooperate in 'relevant working groups' for drafting the rules governing their sectors of interest. If these 'relevant working groups' are anything like the existing 'expert groups' set up by the Commission, they will be made up of at least 90 per cent business representatives. The RCC will foster 'joint submissions' – that is, give US and EU TNCs equal access to the rule-making process. As for relations with the TTIP, 'We'll ask the lawyers' to give us the most watertight legal framework for our purposes, while linking us to the TTIP to make RCC decisions binding and give it treaty-level strength.

The most important news in the paper is that a 'Regulatory Cooperation Council *will* be established' and that this RCC will take over on all the present or future regulations the TTIP can't handle at this stage. This is where the present ambiguity lies.

Some measures would be dangerous to deal with at present because they are too controversial or they will cause an uproar if anything further is leaked – as some parts of some documents inevitably will be. Since the RCC will deal with future regulations as well, it will take over where the TTIP leaves off and will create a permanent rule-making machine, allowing it to become in practice as good or better than a treaty – a 'living agreement'. They will find a judicious way to make it just as legally binding as the treaty itself. At no stage from conception to birth to implementation will the regulatory process escape the tender mercies of the TNCs, which will not be bothered by any trade irritants such as open, democratic processes and procedures.

As usual, such a new institution will be presented as 'purely technical' and as usual will be deeply political. If the governments can get away with it, they will establish the RCC and the mere act of doing so will demonstrate that they know it could prove too tough to ram the TTIP through the barricades as it stands. It hasn't happened as of this writing that I'm aware of, but I would surmise that their next move will be to remove and/or displace a lot of the proposed regulatory changes that both sides of the Atlantic – and both businesses and governments – want, but which rightly alarm citizens. The TNC organizations and complicit governments could make a big PR coup out of this and halt the spread of disagreeable (although perfectly true) rumours concerning the TTIP where regulations are concerned. It would allow negotiators on either side to hand over thorny questions to another non-elected body of 'stakeholders' – we know who that means – to take over the legislative functions of defining regulations governing consumer protection, public health, environmental safety and sustainability, labour law including retirement contributions and many other vitally important issues.

Such a structure could be far better for longer-term corporate interests than leaving regulatory questions in a treaty which the relevant legislative bodies, the European Parliament or the US Congress, could decide to vote down.[9] Elected politicians do not necessarily take kindly to learning that they are about to be stripped of a sizeable portion of their legislative prerogatives. A lot of parliamentary committees would become obsolete. Opponents of the TTIP will have to keep an unblinking eye on BusinessEurope, the US Chamber of Commerce, Commission operatives and *tutti quanti* to see what moves they make next in this direction.

Unfortunately, the lobbies and the Commission all enjoy secrecy and are under no obligation to publish progress reports – 'progress' in the direction they favour, of course. Unless those organizations and elected parliamentarians defending citizens' interests become very good indeed at cultivating internal sources and doing professional, undercover detective work, it's entirely possible that TNC business interests could take over not just the judiciary through ISDS provision, but also a significant share of the legislative function through the RCC.

There are different ways to do this – the point being to gain control over the legislative function to set and approve rules. Business interests, their political allies and their negotiators could put the general rules for 'regulatory cooperation' in the treaty text to make anything they choose to do 'legal' and set up the actual machinery later, in a new 'technical' bureaucracy. They could use the Commission's present exclusive power under existing EU rules to propose legislation (and permanently prevent unwelcome legislation from being proposed by citizens and their elected representatives). They could propose new legislation via the 'comitology procedure' which means there must be a qualified majority of the member governments *against* the proposal in order to reject it.[10] Finding the subtlest, most unchallengeable way to get what you want is, after all, why God made lawyers.

HELPING HANDS

Where regulations are concerned, it is truly convenient that much of the spade work has already been done for the US–EU TNCs, not only by such organizations as the TABD, but also by another little-known outfit in Brussels called the European Risk Forum (ERF).[11] The ERF's singularly uninformative website never tires of repeating that it is an 'expert-led and not-for-profit think-tank that promotes high-quality risk assessment and risk management decisions by the EU institutions'. Their philosophy is that 'risk management decisions should minimise negative, unintended consequences, such as . . . *economic losses, reduced personal freedoms, and restrictions on consumer choice*' (my italics). Who wouldn't want to avoid 'negative, unintended consequences'? But these, like so much other EU-speak, also need decoding. Economic losses for whom? For business, of course (here business would immediately add 'so ultimately for consumers' – that is, for everybody).

Gains for consumers such as those that consist in being able to eat healthy foods, buy cheaper but identical generic medicines, live and breathe in a clean environment, conserve biodiversity and the natural world, benefit from well-maintained public transport networks, drive safe and less polluting automobiles etc. do not enter into the equation of gains and losses – the costs and benefits are seen as purely economic. They don't even concern what economists call 'negative externalities', such as harm caused to people by a polluting factory or to nature by clear-cutting a forest or massive universal dangers such as climate change.

Let me repeat that nobody is against getting rid of, say, time-consuming and unnecessary customs procedures. By all means, eliminate them. Surely plenty of non-contentious duplicate regulations and tests exist: do the same. And it certainly isn't up to me to decide when and when not to use the precautionary principle – this should be the subject of open and public debate.

However, when certain products and processes are suspected or known to present significant risks for human/animal/plant health and safety or for the environment, isn't it normal to use the precautionary principle and ban them, even if the science isn't 100 per cent watertight? Especially when public healthcare and hospitals are still virtually free in EU regimes? Why should taxpayers pay for the freedom of corporations to export hazardous chemicals, medicines or any other potentially dangerous product that can make people ill? Indeed, they, the taxpayers will have to pay the costs of caring for those afflicted by the 'negative, unintended consequences', such as higher rates of illness and disability. A look at rates of obesity in the United States – now well over a third of the American population, with all its attendant diseases – shows one good reason why the US privatized healthcare system is the most costly in the world.

In the USA, lobbies using spurious 'Risk Forum'-type arguments were able to thwart a quite mild campaign in New York City against obesity and diabetes set on reducing consumption of fizzy drinks supersaturated with sugar. All the then Mayor Bloomberg asked was that the largest containers holding just a shade under a half-litre (16 ounces) be banned. The fizzy drinks industry won using an 'astroturf' (see Chapter 1) riposte to argue that this would 'reduce personal freedoms' and 'place restrictions on consumer choice'. The European Risk Forum would surely agree.

Oh, and just offhand, what about the National Rifle Association? Would its members eventually demand, in alliance with US small-arms producers, that Europe allow US exports of handguns, along with their shamelessly lax American standards? If the Europeans refused, would future trade commissioners, the RCC and the European Risk Forum argue that they were

'reducing personal freedoms' and placing 'restrictions on consumer choice'? Sorry, just asking.

Although one can learn little about the ERF from its site,
it's clear that it too is an entirely business-oriented think-tank,
which admits to being largely financed by the 'private sector'.
In its Policy Note 25, the ERF describes a meeting held in
November 2013 under Chatham House Rules.[12] Its distin-
guished guests were invited to 'consider the state of play of
the TTIP negotiations' and to debate 'ways forward'. That in
itself shows that they are given enough information, documents,
meeting minutes and so on to judge that state of play, which is
more than one can say for ordinary people. And that it wants to
go 'forward'. No wonder:

> Invited guests included senior officials from the European
> Commission, the United States Government; United Nations,
> academics, European Parliament, US and EU industry associa-
> tions senior lawyers from leading law firms; representatives of
> EU and of US-based companies; and senior managers from the
> automotive, chemicals, energy, biotechnology, crop protec-
> tion, veterinary medicine, plastics, oil and gas, food and drink,
> personal care, detergent, metals, mining, toy, and pharmaceuti-
> cal sectors.

What could be more balanced and inclusive than that guest list?
Among their several recommendations are – what else? – 'Set
up a new Regulatory Cooperation Council' and 'Establish a
formal mechanism for joint review of future regulations which
could have a significant impact on Trans-Atlantic trade and
investment'.

I could only discern one difference between the ERF's
stance, on the one hand, and, on the other, the earlier,
business-authored call for a RCC or the above-mentioned EU
Commission *Position Paper*. That difference is that the business

people would like to see the RCC doing the entire job, whereas the ERF looks at it more as the body that oversees implementation, made up of senior officials drawn from existing regulatory bodies. It prefers other formal arrangements for the other functions, but the proposals themselves are basically the same.

It's ironic to note that the chairman and the secretary-general of the ERF have quite stunning credentials where risks are concerned. The secretary-general used to occupy the same position at UNICE, the forerunner of BusinessEurope, and formerly worked for various chemical companies. The chairman has been employed by Dow Chemical since 2012, before which he enjoyed a 'long career' at BP.

Risk connoisseurs will appreciate that in 2001 Dow Chemical bought Union Carbide, the company responsible for the 1984 Bhopal gas-cloud disaster in India which, according to official figures (unofficial ones are far higher), caused nearly 4,000 deaths and another 4,000 severe and permanently disabling injuries. Indian plaintiffs have been suing Dow, as they did Union Carbide, for a couple of decades and have got nowhere. The chairman's other previous employer, BP, is the oil company whose monster Deepwater Horizon drilling accident in the Gulf of Mexico in 2011 has been officially blamed by a White House Commission on 'cost-cutting decisions and insufficient safety systems'. The fines and associated expenses have so far cost BP $42 billion. Unintended negative consequences, no doubt.

Finally, the RCC is also slated to interact with 'legislators (US Congress and the European Parliament)'. Which politicians would those be? How reassuring that here, too, we already have just the ticket, provided by another little-known group called the Transatlantic Policy Network, founded in 1992. It brings together some 30 EU and US transnational corporations (Boeing, Citigroup, Coca-Cola, Microsoft, Allianz, Daimler, BP, Syngenta . . .) and legislators, 5 US senators (including four Republicans, of whom two are from Mississippi), 32 members

of the US House of Representatives and, from the EU, 60
MEPs.

They're all there because they favour the TTIP and increased
US–EU cooperation at all levels – commercial, military, judicial,
etc., and seek to increase the scope for action of their respective TNC membership.[13]

Whether they get their way is another question – the answer
depends overwhelmingly on citizen awareness.

4

FROM TRANS- TO SUPRA-NATIONAL: CORPORATE TROOPS INVADE THE UNITED NATIONS

Time to call in the blue helmets: the United Nations needs protection – not from member nations, but from a programme intentionally sheltered within its own walls.

Not content with their influence at the national or at the European level; not satisfied with imposing the most egregiously detrimental transnational treaties in history, the corporate lobbying effort has gone planetary. Could the transatlantic and transpacific trade and investment treaties, TTIP and TTP, actually be mere stepping stones to world management by TNCs and universal authority without accountability? Are such questions paranoid? Political fiction? Perhaps so, perhaps not. You can judge for yourself by checking what the corporations and the private sector have accomplished in just a few years.

In the 1980s and 1990s, the companies became especially attentive to the UN and the increasing number of international conferences its many agencies were holding on the world's most important subjects, such as food and hunger, science and technology, water, habitat, labour and so on. I can personally bear witness to an early manifestation of this interest: the massive presence of agribusiness at the first World Food Conference in Rome in November 1974, where I was surprised and indignant to observe that the corporate delegation was, along with that of the USA, the largest one present.[1]

However, such mass industry participation in UN events from the 1970s to the early 1990s was relatively rare and not systematic. It was only under the leadership of Kofi Annan that it really got under way. Annan was elected UN Secretary-General at the end of 1996 after the United States had vetoed a second term for Boutros Boutros-Ghali. The new Secretary-General took office on 1 January 1997 and served for a full 10 years.[2] Perhaps he did not want to suffer the fate of Boutros-Ghali and sought to please the UN's most powerful member state; in any event he was the first UN Secretary-General to throw open the doors wide and invite the corporations to come in. How best to welcome the private sector in this intergovernmental shrine?

Annan seems to have dreamt up the concept with the then CEO of Nestlé, Helmut Maucher, at a Davos conference, and he launched the idea at the Davos jamboree meeting in January 1999. A year and a half later, the Global Compact had become a formal part of the United Nations (UNGC). Its mission is to organize cooperation between business giants or smaller companies and the UN. Some of us found the actions of the eminent Secretary-General overly solicitous to the TNCs; perhaps we were even overheard referring to him as Neskofi Annan.

But let's be serious. Here is the UNGC's own description of its origins and nature:

Launched in July 2000, the UN Global Compact is a leadership platform for the development, implementation and disclosure of responsible and sustainable corporate policies and practices. Endorsed by chief executives, it seeks to align business operations and strategies everywhere with ten universally accepted principles in the areas of human rights, labour, environment and anti-corruption. With nearly 8,000 corporate participants in over 140 countries, the UN Global Compact is the world's largest voluntary corporate sustainability initiative.[3]

I have no doubt that many businesses are sincere in wanting to promote best practice in the areas of human rights, decent work, environmental sustainability and anti-corruption. So much the better if the UN can encourage their efforts. It costs very little to join the UN programme and put such convictions into practice: UNGC membership is linked to a 'suggested annual voluntary contribution' on a sliding scale: $15,000 for corporations with sales above $5 billion and a mere $250 for those with less than $50 million annual turnover. For such relatively paltry sums, they can decorate their letterheads with the UN logo and meanwhile go after much greater benefits in terms of contacts and public relations.

The UNGC initiative is part of the long line of Corporate Social Responsibility (CSR) ploys which emphasize again and again that companies are quite able to regulate themselves and furthermore are certain to do so since they are upstanding and solid corporate citizens. Again, no doubt that many, if not most, are doing their best.

I remain nonetheless suspicious of CSR wherever it is to be found and promoted. A conference in Austria several years ago was the occasion of my first (and nearly last) participation in any CSR activity. I spoke on the general theme that the first principle of CSR ought to be paying one's full share of taxes so as to support the common good. Companies, wherever they are established, are protected by the police and fire departments, their personnel is educated and cared for by the public school and health systems, their workers arrive at work via well-maintained roads or public transport; their rubbish is collected and their toilets are connected to sewers – all these must be maintained and paid for.

When I had finished my contribution, the man next to me on the platform explained to the audience and to me, as if to a small and not very bright child, that his job was to help corporations to pay the absolute minimum in taxes. From what I have been able to observe, his view has overwhelmingly won out over mine.

The UNGC is a more sophisticated version of CSR: it asks for progress reports from its member companies, but it never monitors either the accuracy of their reports – if they supply them – or their behaviour. Signing on for the 10 principles is enough, and the corporate capacity for self-regulation is unquestioned.

The TNCs that sign on can drape themselves in the UN flag and this leads some critics to accuse them of 'bluewashing'. When one reads the names of some of our old friends in the UNGC membership, such as Coca-Cola (including the HQ in Atlanta and seven subsidiaries), oil and gas giants Total, Shell, BP, plus Nestlé, Unilever, Monsanto and Veolia, it does give one pause.

Certainly, the UNGC has accepted some members of dubious reputation or who have clearly committed human rights and environmental violations – Shell's actions in the Niger Delta in Nigeria and vis-à-vis the Ogoni people come to mind. The UK's mining giants De Beers, Anglo-American and Rio Tinto are present, as are the usual German chemical suspects. Many respectable environmental and humanitarian organizations have joined in denouncing various TNC Global Compact members, but such objections never seem to be considered. Secretary-General Annan himself is said to have personally invited some major companies, including Shell, to join. Perhaps he believed they would get religion by belonging.

In any event, the UNGC requires no proof of progress and it rarely expels a member – this seems to happen only when the company has not paid its voluntary contribution and has shown complete indifference to the programme for several years. Even those in good standing aren't necessarily very fervent about their membership. According to a UNGC report in 2008, 'only 30 per cent of companies with subsidiaries required their regional branches and suppliers to implement the scheme's principles, and only nine per cent of companies with subsidiaries even considered spreading their Compact commitments beyond headquarters'.[4]

Membership also seems rather oddly distributed and hasn't much to do with the relative importance of a country's economy or with its geographical size and population. Out of the thousands of member companies, France has the most, at more than a thousand. Next comes Brazil (595), then the USA (553), followed by several with 300-some (China, Germany, India, the United Kingdom). Italy has 218 members, little Switzerland 147 and enormous Russia 76.

Certainly, the activities of the UNGC help to build and reinforce the Davos Class if only because the Compact is truly international, as opposed to such annual Masters of the Universe gatherings as the Bilderberg Group meetings, which remain pretty much pure white Western love-fests. 'Latinos are no good at this sort of thing', a journalist from the French newspaper *Libération* reported overhearing a participant say as he left the Parisian site of one of Bilderberg's closed-to-the-press meetings. For the UNGC, on the contrary, a Latino or African billionaire businessman is just as good as an American one.

The UNGC brings together not only the Masters of the Universe, but also many aspiring Davos devotees. A long report on the Global Compact 2013 'Leaders Summit and Private Sector Forum' (LEAD) held in New York provides a good example, with several dozen prestigious invitees shown in large photos and some 1,100 or 1,200 participants – almost all corporate – listed on 50 pages. At such events, the less illustrious attendees can at least figuratively rub shoulders with the likes of Ban Ki Moon and the Queen of Belgium, African presidents (Nigeria, Benin), UN agency heads (UNESCO, UNDP), ex-Prime Ministers (Gordon Brown) and assorted CEOs or government ministers. It's good training for apprentices striving for future Davos Class membership.

When Kofi Annan first created the Global Compact, the only UN agencies involved were related to the 10 principles: environment (UNEP); labour (ILO) and human rights (UN High Commission for Refugees, UNHCR). Later, the Secretary-General sent instructions from headquarters to all UN member agencies that they were each to provide a high-level representative to liaise with UNGC member companies and facilitate interaction with them. Now, virtually every UN agency, whatever its specialty, has one or several contact people to welcome its corporate membership.

Meanwhile, there have been other corporate incursions into the UN, whether the perpetrators have been UNGC members or not. A good example is the cash-strapped World Health Organization (WHO). Some UN agencies have fixed budgets that come from New York HQ or fixed member state contributions – others, particularly specialized agencies such as WHO, must make do with voluntary or special emergency donations. This has left them open to Public–Private Partnerships (PPPs) with organizations that may be far more partial to the Private than to the Public side of the equation.

This financial penury is the context of Bill Gates's invitation to be special guest speaker at the 2005 annual WHO World Health Assembly (WHA). He was asked back in 2011 for a repeat performance: to give the keynote speech for the WHA. This was not to everyone's liking. The People's Health Movement, an NGO collective of health professionals, specialists and activists who fight for free and universal public health systems, saw Gates's presence as part of an alarming trend of various UN organizations, including WHO, kowtowing to global multinational corporations under the guise of the 'Global Compact' and so-called 'Public–Private Partnerships'. [A People's Health spokesperson added], 'It's time to either declare Microsoft a WHO member country, or stop the shameful promotion of global corporations at important UN meetings.'[5]

Melinda Gates nonetheless keynoted the Assembly in 2014. The Gateses might reply they were present as co-chairs of their Foundation, the richest charity in the world with more than $38 billion in assets as of 2013 and a munificent funder of health and vaccination campaigns. Politely, they did not remind those present that between 1999 and 2007, the Gates Foundation, among a number of other whopping multimillion dollar grants to health programmes, gave a cumulative total of nearly $337 million directly to the same WHO.

One can thus understand that Margaret Chan, Director of the WHO, felt that some sign of recognition would not be amiss and that a keynote speech was a small gesture to make in return. Decent manners in sum. Quite so, but being a charity doesn't necessarily mean that all its impacts will be favourable, particularly for local people. In *Whose Crisis, Whose Future?* I tried to show why another of Gates's undertakings, the Alliance for a Green Revolution for Africa (AGRA), was the epitome of the 'technological fix' and certain to devastate the lives of smaller, more vulnerable food producers. The aim of AGRA, in its own words, is to 'create a policy environment favourable to market-driven, export-oriented agriculture', putting the accent on GMO seeds, greater use of chemical fertilizers and pesticides and reliance on purchased inputs.

The real need in Africa is for food production, not cash crops, based on bio – not biotech – and eco-farming that is labour-intensive and relies on natural, cost-free techniques.

One such technique now being introduced in Malawi is to plant three species of trees – which fix the soil and fix water – and to use selectively their leaves, crushed, as fertilizer or insect repellents for food crops. Many other such tricks of the trade are being revived or invented and cost little or nothing.[6] By definition, these methods are available to small farmers who more often than not in Africa are women.

Such techniques prevent the farmer from being locked into purchases of seeds and other inputs every season. Comparative tests on hundreds of thousands of hectares in widely different geographical settings have shown Africa's land and people to be entirely capable of doubling harvests using eco-farming (also termed agroecology) alone. This doesn't mean that such farming is 'primitive' – actually it's based on implicit or explicit scientific findings and is far more sophisticated than using GMOs and chemicals. What's more, it has stood the tests of time and evolution. The bugs have read Darwin, whereas it appears that the GMO lab-scientists have not: pests quickly adapt to chemical pesticides and come back even stronger after just a few generations.

However, eco-oriented farming has one big problem. It makes no money for anyone – at least not for anyone who counts. All it does is feed the producer and her family and benefit those who buy their food at local markets, whereas AGRA will benefit TNCs such as Monsanto, of which Gates owns quite a lot of stock. Vandana Shiva, the well-known Indian campaigner for biodiversity and peasant agriculture, does not mince words and has termed the Gates Foundation 'the greatest threat to farmers in the developing world'.[7]

Now it looks as though the Gates Foundation's activities in medicine might be just as questionable as those in the agricultural arena. Naturally, any person, any institution with as much money as Gates, is going to be the target of criticism. Nobody's perfect, etc. etc.

The fact remains that in spite of the nice sound of PPPs Public–Private Partnerships will have irreconcilable conflicts of interest. Those fighting for universal public health systems are worried not just by the trend towards privatization, but also by the massive presence of so-called 'civil society' – read 'business' – lobby groups that are popping up everywhere, particularly in WHO and other UN meetings. Since WHO is chronically underfunded, it can only welcome another PPP initiative – the Global Fund to Fight HIV/AIDS, Tuberculosis and Malaria.

The Global Fund was set up in the early 2000s by successive decisions of the G-8 and receives heaps of Gates Foundation money. It is a financing, not an implementing organization; it appears to be well managed and funds both government and private programmes, so it's hard to criticize the corporate presence. It also measures its success in *numbers* – how many people taking retroviral drugs, how many insecticide-treated mosquito nets distributed and so on, so businesses are attracted to it because it assumes any ordinary human problems away. Therefore, the people taking the drugs can do so with clean water, have easy access to renewing their supply, don't have a government spreading the rumour that vaccinations are anti-fertility doses in disguise, and so on. The Global Fund also reinforces the idea that PPPs are the 'new normal' way to deal with public health, while never challenging pharmaceutical companies or profit-making hospitals.

In September 2011, the UN General Assembly held a high-level meeting to deal with the biggest killer diseases of all. These are non-communicable diseases such as heart disease, cancer, stroke, diabetes, respiratory illnesses and the like. They are responsible for nearly two-thirds of all deaths, including those in the poor countries – the difference with the rich ones being that when you live in a poor country, you're much more likely to die from one of them before you reach the age of 60. On the list of civil society invitees to this UN meeting were a great many legitimate public health-oriented organizations in UN member states, but also such industry lobby umbrella groups as the International Food and Beverage Association, the International Federation of Pharmaceutical Manufacturers Associations, the Global Alcohol Producers Group, the Global Business Coalition on HIV/AIDS, Tuberculosis and Malaria – plus a good many individual pharmaceutical or other corporate representatives and the omnipresent WEF, aka Davos.

Their attendance prompted more than 100 NGOs and medical groups to petition the UN, deploring 'a lack of clarity of roles for the industry sector in UN health policy setting and shaping' and calling for a binding code of conduct for the corporations.[8] One of the signatories, Patti Rundall, who as co-chair of the International Baby Foods Action Network (IBFAN) has been tirelessly active against the baby formula marketers for more than 30 years, explained that 'Partnership isn't the right word. It implies trust and respect. The allegiance of the food companies is to create profits. Their voluntary commitments are only good for as long as they want to keep them.'[9]

After all these years, IBFAN is still at it. So, on the opposite side, are the baby-formula TNCs, and Margaret Chan is still WHO Director. As of March 2014, IBFAN was again speaking out against a new WHO policy proposal which runs counter to Chan's frequent claims that WHO activities and policies must be protected from corporate influence. And yet, according to these opponents, she is presently calling for 'Official Relations Status' to be conferred on international business associations. Such a new designation would give them legitimate front row seats at WHO's governing body meetings where they could lobby to their hearts' content.

A lot of them used to attend the meetings anyway and lobbied *sub rosa*, but they first had to worm their way in via membership in an official state delegation or by forming fake NGOs. Pretty soon they may be able to attend with heads held high. Including business among the delegates would make WHO's governing bodies public–private entities; the corporations would also be authorized to establish 'three-year plans' with WHO. IBFAN pertinently asks 'Will WHO prefer to engage in partnerships with corporations . . . or will WHO help Member States bring in legally binding controls that truly protect the right to health of their citizens?'[10]

At the prompting of Kofi Annan, from the year 2000, several UN specialized agencies also developed their own private corporate partnership arrangements using their own guidelines. UNICEF (children's health), for example, excludes infant formula manufacturers, but there has been no overall UN judgment or guidelines on which private sectors or corporations are eligible or ineligible to attend meetings. Given the existence of the UNGC at headquarters, it seems unlikely that any guidelines, much less the exclusion of individual corporations, can happen any time soon.

HAPPY BUSINESS DAY TO YOU

Ever since the first initiatives of Kofi Annan, corporate presence inside the UN has been growing and branching out. The UN Environment Programme (UNEP) has been a particularly warm-hearted host, to the point that specific 'business days' are now set aside in intergovernmental environment conferences or joint corporate–government preparatory meetings. These days are designed not just to allow corporate brass to sing 'happy business day to us' and encourage everyone to applaud; they are also serious transnational encounters to better prepare or magnify the corporate input. Sad to report, the companies' presence has been extremely effective. The World Business Council for Sustainable Development (WBCSD) – another haven for about 200 major TNCs – has been an active partner alongside UNGC.[11] The WBCSD has become a kind of UNEP alter ego or doppelgänger.

Massive business presence has changed both the context and the concepts embodied in the UN's relationship to the environment. The specialised agency UNEP was founded in 1972 and was a welcome sign that the UN took environmental problems seriously. In 1987, following increasingly alarming scientific reports on the damage that chlorofluorocarbons (CFCs) were doing to the ozone layer, UNEP pushed through the Montreal Protocol, which was duly ratified and entered into force in 1989. Since then, CFCs have been banned and chemical damage to the ozone shield has been halted or reversed. This unprecedented international success was no thanks to DuPont – the US chemical giant that founded the Alliance for Responsible CFC Policy (great PR name, that) – which argued that the science was too full of holes to warrant any action. DuPont's board chair was quoted as saying that ozone depletion theory is 'a science fiction tale ... a load of rubbish ... utter nonsense', and its spokesperson testified to the US Congress in 1987 that 'there is no immediate crisis that demands unilateral regulation'. DuPont and its corporate CFC producer Alliance lost, big time, and the Montreal Protocol is still seen by many as the greatest international environmental victory ever achieved.[12]

So the UN at one time was to some degree the 'house of the peoples', as in 'We the peoples of the United Nations', not the house of corporations and their lobbies. It welcomed a great many civil society organizations which were able to participate or at least to observe its activities. It still does, but the NGOs today are often shunted to a site miles from the place where the real action takes place. Large corporations used to be seen as either somewhat suspicious or irrelevant to UN activities. Now they set the agenda for many of them. In addition to health, the domain of climate and environment is probably the area in which they have made the greatest inroads.

The ground-breaking UN Conference on Environment and Development (UNCED), informally called the 'Earth Summit', held in in Rio di Janeiro in June 1992, was a watershed event. The big topics under discussion included replacing fossil fuels with alternative energy sources, strategies against dangerous chemicals, toxic products and wastes, as well as increasing public transport while reducing automobile emissions and the like. At Rio 1992, the Climate Change Convention was signed that eventually gave birth to the United Nations Framework Convention on Climate Change (UNFCC) and the Kyoto Protocol. The legally binding Convention on Biodiversity was another milestone; in all, 2,400 NGO representatives were present and their parallel Global Forum brought together 17,000 people. The forum exerted a lot of pressure on the officials, goading them to advance on a genuine environmental agenda, and it obtained 'consultative status'. How could big business possibly appreciate such an agenda?

The rich countries that – it had been decided – were supposed to provide additional financial resources for the poor ones didn't appreciate it much either. They never accepted the bedrock principle of 'common but differentiated responsibility' for tackling climate change. Much backsliding occurred and no action was taken to curb the behaviour of TNCs that were out in the world grabbing up natural resources and increasing their CO_2 emissions. Largely at the initiative of the United States, the only UN agency that might have kept the idea of controlling the corporations alive was closed down within a year after Rio. This was the UN Centre on Transnational Corporations, which had been working on a binding code of conduct. It was destroyed at a stroke, swatted down by Uncle Sam.

By the early 1990s, the initial phase of globalization was in full swing and the companies were growing bolder and demanding deregulation. As Martin Khor, then director of the Third World Network, now head of the intergovernmental South Centre in

Geneva, commented presciently in his 1997 assessment of the Earth Summit five years on:

> Since it is most unlikely that businesses will voluntarily curb their own practices so as to be in line with sustainable development, especially since there is now an intensification of competition, the removal of the rights of states to regulate business, especially TNCs, is a *major and perhaps fatal flaw* in the international community's attempt to arrest environmental deterioration and promote sustainable development.[13]

Indeed, the companies have never looked back. Since the Earth Summit, where they had almost no presence except via their governments, they have gained more and more traction.

By the time of 'Rio+10', held in Johannesburg in 2002, corporations were larger, they had invested more abroad, their main activity was still resource plunder and they were much better prepared. They also had George W. Bush in the White House and the TNCs, American or not, were flexing their muscles. Ten years after the first Earth Summit, the 1992 statement of Maurice Strong, the wealthy Canadian businessman and industrialist who had served as Secretary-General at the Rio Conference, also seemed prophetic: 'The environment is not going to be saved by environmentalists. Environmentalists do not hold the levers of economic power.'[14]

As if to illustrate this statement, the George W. Bush administration decided not to send a delegation to Johannesburg in 2002, and this stole some of the corporate thunder. But it also gave those present the opportunity to stave off any new proposals for binding codes of conduct or binding conventions like the one on biodiversity or the Forest Principles that had been approved in Rio 10 years earlier. Johannesburg thus also consolidated a largely invisible victory for the TNCs.

As Khor noted, the biggest mistake of the Rio Summit in

1992 had been the decision not to seek a mechanism to regulate corporations, which, shortly after Rio, also began to benefit mightily from the new rules imposed by the WTO, which came upon the scene in 1995. Patents owned by TNCs suddenly became good for 20 years minimum, slowing down technology transfer to the poor countries. Rules for trade in goods and services opened up access to new markets in which small local companies couldn't compete with the giants. Deregulation of the inflows or outflows of foreign capital destabilized many governments. Developing countries' foreign debt grew and they had to pay it back in hard currency earned by overexploiting their resources and exporting them. All this took a toll on the environment as well.

By the time the Rio+20 UN environmental conference arrived, the TNCs were far stronger than they had been in 1992 or 2002 – they were no longer just passively benefitting, but were in charge of the agenda. They made up the largest delegation to Rio and their concepts were the only ones seriously discussed. They also staged the largest event, known as 'Business Day'. The UNGC, WBCSD, International Chamber of Commerce and others brought the troops out.[15]

Here, the permanent representative of the UN International Chamber of Commerce (yes, like a country's permanent representative) declared to thunderous applause, 'We are . . . the largest business delegation ever to attend a UN Conference . . . Business needs to take the lead and we **are** taking the lead.'[16]

The TNCs have now secured an all-but formal role in UN climate negotiations. They have framed the discussions so that their concept of the green economy is paramount. It assumes that there is a market solution to any problem and that nature can be measured and valued according to the 'services' it provides (for example, cleaning water, capturing carbon and so on). In this way, nature's services can be given a price, offset and traded on markets via credits, similar to carbon trading

– despite the fact that carbon trading has been completely unsuccessful in regulating emissions and has provided windfall profits to companies. UNEP now argues that putting a price tag on nature is the best way to protect it.

Perhaps UNEP will be kind enough to tell us what would be the cost of a world without bees and whether the TNCs suspected of killing them off should be admitted to environmental conferences. Perhaps in some utopian future the UNGC will apply cost-benefit analysis to its membership and decide whether the human rights violators and ecological felons guilty of crimes against the earth should be requested to leave.

BURN BABY BURN

The ambiguity surrounding so many TNCs has become literally insufferable in some quarters – for example, in the case of the November 2013 annual Climate Conference, formally the UN Framework Conference on Climate Change (UNFCC), held in Warsaw.[17]

One hardly knows whether to call it the Climate Conference or the Coal Conference – in fact it was both. The Polish government simultaneously convened the UNFCC and the so-called International Coal and Climate Summit on behalf of the World Coal Association. As most people surely know by now, coal is the most CO_2-intensive, polluting fossil fuel there is, and it is notoriously the largest single source of greenhouse gas pollution in the world. The conference theme, 'clean coal', was a fairytale because there is no such thing and won't be for many a year, if ever. It does not seem to have struck Polish officialdom that running COP 19 and the International Coal and Climate Summit in parallel could be interpreted as sheer provocation. Nor did it bother the head of UNFCC since 2010, Christiana Figueres, who gave the keynote speech for the Coal Conference – the business one – thus succeeding in enraging even the mildest of the NGOs present; 1,600 NGOs were accredited observers, of which 150, accompanied by the representatives of the Least Developed Countries, staged a walkout in Warsaw – unprecedented but fully warranted.[18]

For the first time in the history of UNFCC annual conferences, a government (Poland) called for corporate sponsorship and got it – from Arcelor-Mittal and BMW among others. Arcelor, the steel giant, paid for building all the conference structures and got its logo on the big tent, erected inside the Warsaw sports stadium. BMW (which has lobbied incessantly to lower emissions standards for automobiles), provided cars; General Motors (well known for funding climate change denialist think-tanks in the USA) supplied vans, the Polish oil and gas LOTOS group gave delegates 11,000 tote-bags displaying its logo and – of course – the coal industry occupied the place of honour.

Poland depends on coal for nearly 90 per cent of its power supply and brazenly associated coal with solving rather than aggravating the problem. Nor did the Polish Ministry of Economy abstain from issuing a joint communiqué with its environmental colleague to announce that their Summit brought together 'the leadership of the world's largest coal-producing companies, senior policy makers, business leaders, academics and NGO representatives' who are said to have agreed that climate protection is possible, 'while allowing coal to continue to play its role as an affordable, abundant, easily accessible source of energy'. The coal industry will naturally continue to seek 'more efficient coal technologies to tackle climate change', including the mythical clean coal produced with new combustion technologies, plus 'carbon capture and storage', but most experts advise that neither of these will be ready for significant use for another 15 years, if then.[19]

At this stage, it seems fair to say that the United Nations has become part of the problem that citizens face in attempting to deal with the world's manifold ills – economic or climatic. The UNGC is not an ally: it has never proposed anything but 'voluntary guidelines' for companies; no evidence shows that membership in the UNGC has had the slightest impact on corporate behaviour or on business priorities worldwide. Why should there be? The UNGC never sanctions a member company, no matter what it does.

Figueres, an important personage at the UN, was not obliged to give the keynote speech for the International Coal and Climate Summit, in which she 'endorsed the role of the coal industry in any future climate deal' and put the United Nations on record as supporting these climate culprits. The UNGC was not obliged to open the door to the gradual TNC infiltration of virtually all UN programmes and specialized agencies. It has never suggested any solution to any world problem except for proposing unspecified voluntary measures to be taken by 'enlightened companies'.

We need strict, enforceable rules and binding laws – preferably international – governing corporate behaviour, not fake solutions. We need thorough housecleaning rather than cossetting of companies at UN headquarters. But since the United States can still make or break nominations for Secretary-General, it is probable we shall continue to have smiling, pliable and ineffectual Secretary-Generals forever, unless citizens choose to make the UN and its Global Compact particular targets. Alas, citizens' means are limited, and the number of crises to confront is already huge.

However, for climate conferences, the UNFCC-COP is still the only game in town internationally speaking and it would be a mistake for NGOs to halt their forceful lobbying at successive COPs. That would accomplish nothing and would leave the field even clearer for corporate lobbying. Coal is notoriously the largest single source of greenhouse gas pollution in the world. Realistically, given our forces and our treasuries, the UNGC will probably continue to push its senseless and useless 'solutions', prolonging the fiction of Corporate Social Responsibility. But at least we can 'name and shame'; we can continue to denounce the deadly combination of greenwashing – 'we the TNCs are environmental saviours' – and bluewashing as they are allowed to drape themselves in the UN flag, discrediting the entire institution.

5

DAVOS: DESIGNER OF THE FUTURE?

I wish we were at the end of this story, and probably you do as well – too much bad news in a single gulp is hard on the digestion – but there is still one more thing to tell about the growing grip of neoliberal transnational business interests on the affairs of everyone else. The most visionary and farsighted among them want to do something quite simple: run the world.

Personally, I marvel at the hubris on display which seems completely unconscious, simply the normal attitude for the can-do businessman or woman. Recall the 'Approved Once, Accepted Everywhere' slogan of the Transatlantic Business Dialogue, or the way the TTIP and the new regulators have planned to usurp the judiciary and privatize a good part of the legislative and executive powers of democratic governments in order to replace them with their self-selected arbiters and 'experts'. Maybe they assume they can and should always get their way because they're more efficient than the rest of us. They sense they can proceed without hindrance because people don't understand what's happening or because they're already accustomed to the corporate onslaught and feel it's inevitable.

Perhaps worse, the TNCs see no reason why private and public, for-profit and non-profit activities can't inhabit exactly the same sphere. For the Davos Class, those who think private and public should be kept separate, with democratic governments making the rules – people such as the present author – have simply missed the bus and the zeitgeist.

On this subject, here is an anecdote about President Bill Clinton. Was he joking or serious?

The scene is the presidential plane AirForce One. Clinton is chatting with the journalists on board and tells them he's reading a great book called *Global Dreams* about how the most powerful transnational corporations control the world. A journalist asks him, 'What are you going to do about this, Mr. President?' 'What am I going to do about it? Nothing. I'm only the President of the United States. I can't do anything about these companies.'[1]

Statement of fact? Self-deprecating humour? If the first, he's confessing helplessness; if the second, he's signifying his passive acceptance or absence of political will. In either case, if a political leader who is or was 'only' the president of the largest economy and most powerful country on earth feels helpless or unwilling to touch the TNCs, what can be said of lesser leaders? The European heads of state all rushed in herd formation to sign the TTIP mandate, a text carefully prepared by the TNCs. France alone asked for a minor change before signing – to leave audiovisual products and services out of the treaty.

Are governments really that scared? That blind? That lazy? Or simply in total agreement with the neoliberal corporate agenda? Are the TNCs really invincible? Is it true that nothing can be done – indeed, that nothing *should* be done? This isn't certain, but it *is* certain that the companies have a more unified vision and are better organized among themselves than governments, much less the social forces that might oppose them.

Despite all the G-8s, G-20s and G-whatnots over the past 20 years; despite any number of international organizations in which governments have the opportunity to build alliances and coalitions: they have never developed anything approaching the close-knit class consensus that exists between, say, BusinessEurope, the US Chamber of Commerce, the International Chamber of Commerce, the European Roundtable of Industrialists, the World Business Council for Sustainable Development and many others. Wherever governments gather – for example, the richer ones in the OECD or the poorer in the G-77 or all of them together in the UN – they have rarely, if ever, forged any common demands. The highly developed states, whether oriented centre-right or centre-left, have increasingly sided with the 'business community'. They have not even got together to defend their essential prerogatives as governments, such as keeping an independent judiciary. Transnational business, on the other hand, knows exactly what it wants. It has also become far more aggressive in its demands, as we've seen, I hope, again and again in these pages.

Until a couple of decades ago, in the same way Bill Clinton was saying 'I can't do anything about these companies', the companies were figuratively saying, 'we can't do anything about these governments – at least not all of them at once'. But now the World Economic Forum – Davos – the institution that brings together the most transnational corporations as well as a great many governments, in its unofficial Swiss mountain eyrie and its other far-flung international meeting places, is changing the game.

It has devised an ambitious – no, a grandiose, a super-hubristic – plan to set the agenda, to take over where governments leave off, accomplish what they leave out, decide on the issues they won't touch. For the first time, the corporate leadership is saying in a single, loud voice: 'Whatever needs doing can be done by private corporations and done far better than by governments.' And it would seem that an enormous amount needs doing.

To carry out this plan, they have both a pilot project and a vehicle: the worldwide Davos network and its Global Redesign Initiative (GRI). This GRI is a vast and daring programme geared to replacing old, worn-out government multilateralism with an entirely new concept of global governance. The strategy and the ideology behind it could be called 'multi-stakeholder-ism'; it is based on intricate webs of 'multi-stakeholders' and draws upon a 600-page blueprint entitled *Everybody's Business: Strengthening International Cooperation in a More Interdependent World*.[2]

If you find the mere mention of 600 pages depressing, let me say that I certainly didn't read them all, although I believe it would be worth doing. There is surely much of value here and 1,200 experts were involved. The structure is nothing if not thorough. If you choose to study the GRI report more closely, the table of contents gives the nine overarching topics and the list of the Global Agenda Councils (GACs) that figure under each of these broad topics. These GACs – 46 in all – are working groups charged with making concrete proposals. Here are the nine big headings, with the number of GACs working on them in parentheses:

1 Creating a Values Framework (8)
2 Building Sustained Economic Growth (5)
3 Strengthening the International Monetary and Financial System (3)
4 Creating Employment, Eradicating Poverty and Improving Social Welfare (6)
5 Managing and Mitigating Global Risks (7)
6 Ensuring Health for All (4)
7 Enhancing Global Security (4)
8 Ensuring Sustainability (10, plus 7 'Low-Carbon Prosperity Task Forces')
9 Building Effective Institutions in an Empowered Society (4).

You can also take the quick route to a two-page spread with 42 pictures capturing the subjects Davos people think they should be dealing with.[3]

The ambition is breathtaking. Click on any of the pictures and you will discover that they are generally grouped in the main categories as above and that each of these has subcategories which usually have sub-subcategories such as 'partners', which invite further investigation, which in turn . . . But enough. It's a complex, costly and serious undertaking; the WEF is calling on – it would seem – just about every corporation and institution that has ever crossed the threshold of the Davos January jamboree as well as many that haven't.

So with all these intended good works of obvious merit, plus the Davos 'strap line' – 'Committed to Improving the State of the World' – that appears on all its documents, who could be churlish enough not to sign on? Why am I being such a spoilsport, writing yet another critical chapter about a handsomely financed initiative that surely must be out to do its best to change all our lives for the better? Am I guilty of wanting to worsen the state of the world, which I agree is already pretty awful?

I plead guilty. I do not want the Davos Class to be in charge of improving the world. At the beginning of this book I explained why I hate the word 'stakeholder' and when 'multi' is prefixed to it, I hate it even more. This said, I feel one should give Klaus Schwab, the guiding light of Davos from its inception in 1971, credit (or blame, as you will) for foisting this concept upon us. Schwab is German and Germans are dogged, if I may be forgiven a national stereotype. The point is that he has won. After 40 years, the term has become omnipresent; it's embedded in the European Commission and in many other contexts.[4] The concept of stakeholder has its roots in business, as in the following passage from the Davos 40-year history shows:

> [T]he management of an enterprise is not only accountable to
> its shareholders but must also serve the interests of all stake-
> holders, including employees, customers, suppliers and, more
> broadly, government, civil society and any others who may be
> affected or concerned by its operations.[5]

The term has now become eminently political and has gradually replaced 'citizen'. This is convenient for masking or glossing
over hard truths and I can't help praising the Global Redesign
people for their invariably soothing, bland and rich vocabulary.
Let me tell you, these people can write!

Here is a sampling of their prose:

- 'wider international community . . . more pre-emptive and
  coordinated action'
- 'expand the geometry of cooperation to capitalise on the
  wider availability of non-state expertise and resources'
- 'creating new international law and resources'
- 'integrating non-governmental expertise . . . and resources
  into policy frameworks and implementation'
- 'multi-stakeholder coalitions of the willing and able'
- 'multidimensionality rather than multilateralism alone is
  the strategy that emerges from the work of the Global
  Redesign process'
- 'a new stakeholder paradigm of international governance
  analogous to corporate governance'.

These snippets are all, ever so politely and gently, saying one
thing: Move Over and Get Out of the Way. Governments have
fallen short and a lot more involvement of business in running
world affairs is called for. Perhaps a few other groups or individuals in 'civil society' will have a small role to play, but they will
be hand-picked by the powerful players; they may or may not be
representative of the real world of trade unions, small business

federations, nongovernmental organizations, charities, cooperatives, social movements and other not-for-profit endeavours.

The new multi-stakeholders may or may not pay attention
to what 'ordinary people' think and you can rest assured that
anyone invited to join a Davos undertaking will have no past
record of upsetting any apple-carts. Some non-profits will
certainly, if asked, come running in hopes of 'changing them
from within' and also because benefits could come out of the
deal. When the goal is stated as 'creating new international law
and resources; integrating non-governmental expertise . . . and
resources into policy frameworks and implementation', this is
catnip for your average middle of the road NGO leader, especially the part about 'resources'.[6]

In other words, neither I, nor 90% per cent of my friends, nor
most people I know professionally need apply. We might say
something awkward or be perceived as uncooperative. Those
invited from 'civil society', except when that means 'business',
will in any case never be the convenors of the meetings and
the activities, nor will they set the agendas. They have fewer
resources, they may or may not be called upon to ratify the
decisions of those in the group who end up making them and
they might, or might not, be involved with the execution of
whatever is decided or in a position to evaluate the results.

What might be decided, by whom, on the basis of which
proposals? Dozens of them can be found in the huge GRI report
Everybody's Business. Many are perfectly sensible and useful.
What is complicated is figuring out which ones will become
priorities. Which will be further winnowed, refined and elabo-
rated, by whom; who will 'sell' them to governments and to the
other 'stakeholders'? There are no guarantees that these steps
will be taken by the same people who drew them up to begin
with; that is, by the experts who figure on the lists of each of the
GAC members. Furthermore, on the copyright page at the very
beginning of the Davos report, we can read:

The various views expressed in this report do not necessarily reflect those of the Patron Governments. Nor do the various views expressed in this report necessarily reflect those of all the Global Agenda Council Members, Industry Partner communities or Young Global Leader Task Forces, nor do they represent an institutional position of the World Economic Forum or its Members.

So whose views do they reflect?

For example, three GACs figure under the major heading 'Strengthening the International Financial and Monetary System' which concern Global Investment Flows, the International Monetary System and Systemic Financial Risk. Of 19 participants in the Global Investment Flows group, 12 are from business, 5 from universities or think-tanks and 3 are public officials. (I give double membership to the CEO of the National Bank of Kuwait, who is also chair of the Arab Business Council of the WEF.)

The International Monetary System GAC is balanced quite differently – it includes only three business people with eight university and five public figures – including the number two official at the International Monetary Fund and the Chief Economist at the World Bank. One of those academics is John Williamson, the economist who more or less invented and codified the *Washington Consensus* policy, better known to indebted governments as 'structural adjustment' or just plain belt-tightening Austerity. These neoliberal policies are widely acknowledged (for example, by many officials in the UN Development Programme) as responsible for 'the lost decade for development' in the South of the 1980s.[7]

The GAC on Systemic Financial Risk is not, at least for me, particularly reassuring, given its nine finance industry people and several economists, none of whom saw the 2007–8 crisis coming.[8] This GAC is chaired by a former Goldman Sachs high-flyer – apparently the only woman in the group.

I also find it worrisome that the GACs on Food Security and on Nutrition have opened the doors wide to the giant food and commodities agribusiness Bunge, to the CEO of General Mills and the Chairman of Unilever, along with a major Brazilian agribusiness centre and the Gates Foundation's AGRA programme, discussed earlier in these pages. The Nutrition GAC includes Coca-Cola, PepsiCo and Nestlé.

The initiative on Water Pathways 2030 – *A Platform to Accelerate Local Progress of Water Sector Reform* – emanates from the Water Security GAC and is surely one of the more advanced. It already has projects start-ups going in different parts of the world (Mexico, South Africa, for example) and has a 12-member steering board, all of which are TNCs, including Coca-Cola, Dow Chemical Nestlé, PepsiCo, Standard Chartered Bank, Syngenta and Unilever.

The GRI worked intensely from 2009 to 2011, when it published its mammoth report, but was by no means closed down. The work of producing the 600-page study is now over, but the enterprise itself continues today in many guises and is to be found acting in many places, always internationally. Since then, the number of people involved in the GACs has grown by a third, from 1,200 to 1,600, and the number of GACs themselves has doubled to more than 80. An annual meeting, 'the world's largest brainstorming', is hosted by the United Arab Emirates and a steady stream of reports and updates issues from WEF Headquarters. The notion of multi-stakeholder undertakings is becoming part of the international language and scenery. 'Partnership' is the new word for annexation. Make no mistake: governments, including intergovernmental structures, need and apparently welcome the infusion of new energy from the private sector. This is the template for the future.

Davos itself is the world's most successful multi-stakeholder enterprise and the GRI is a planet-sized, giant, permanent Davos January love-fest with self-selected players doing the thinking, the designing and the implementing. If this model continues to advance, as it shows every sign of doing, voting will not be out-lawed – these people are not fools – but it will become largely superfluous except for local concerns. For global 'governance' – here we approach the full significance of that dreaded word – the private sector will be paramount.

The initial funding for this vast undertaking came from the governments of Qatar, Singapore, Switzerland and Tanzania, and it's a safe bet to assume Tanzania wasn't the main financial sponsor. Tiny Qatar, on the other hand, clearly wants to be a global player. This ambition is expressed through activities as consensual as football (the Paris Saint-Germain club) and world-class museums, to the most dis-sensual, such as arming Syrian rebels, including jihadists, and lending one's territory to the US military as the base for all its actions in the Persian Gulf and the launching pad for the 2003 invasion of Iraq. Although Qatar also sponsors peace talks in hotspots as fraught as Darfur, its labour laws forbid its foreign workers (85 per cent of the population) to leave or change their job without the employers' permission. The Emir has the final say on everything that happens in the country, which has held no legislative elections since 1970.

So it sounds like a pretty compatible choice and mutual ben-efit society for the GRI, where democracy isn't very welcome either.

Singapore and Switzerland can be counted on for financial backing too, as they are at the top of the world's wealth per capita list, while Tanzania provides a bit of third world veneer. Now the United Arab Emirates, another geographically small, financially large middle-Eastern power, has joined the club.

The WEF began the GRI process in 2009 with its 1,200 invited experts and the massive Davos Bible that emerged from their work. The recommendations all stem from the 'multi-stakeholder model', which can neatly fit into the free market as well as include selected friendly governments and leaders of civil society. In the fullness of time, the aim appears to be to replace or deeply alter most of the UN's specialized agencies. The Global Compact, as illustrated in the preceding chapter, is both a kind of Trojan horse and an initial testing ground for a far more ambitious policy that could make the United Nations a joint venture with the transnationals and carefully selected civil society organizations. Now we can see the full scope of Kofi Annan's long-term vision when he set up the UNGC.

It's perfectly true that intergovernmental and UN processes can be maddeningly slow, but does that justify stripping them of most of their influence in international affairs? Harris Gleckman and David Sogge[9] identify five areas vital to democracy that are politely ignored by the WEF's report. Most of the 'multi-stakeholder activities' will take place in a transborder, not a national context. I paraphrase and amend Gleckman and Sogge's observations:

- Corporations are not accountable to citizens anywhere now, so if states withdraw from (or are pushed out of) broad geographical and sectoral areas, accountability will disappear altogether. How will we even know what issues they have chosen to work on? Farewell to transparency.
- Sectors labelled Business and Civil Society are vast and varied: who decides on whom to invite to deliberate on what and according to which criteria? Adieu as well to any hopes of fair selection of participants and the constituencies they represent.
- If the Global Compact template is any guide, stakeholders will be free to choose the activities they want to participate in, for as much or little time as they like, on whatever ad hoc basis they choose, there's little hope for effective management. Davos thinks voluntarism is part of the solution – others would see it as part of the problem.
- How are decisions made? Clearly not by ballots cast by

qualified voters. By 'consensus'? This can mean by the richest and most powerful who can coerce weaker members. Who ratifies and validates? The same people who brought about the decision? The GRI proposes no model of decision-making.

- Money. Who pays for whom to participate? The UN's budget is shrinking inexorably. The selected governments, if any, can presumably pay their way but most NGOs are too poor to send representatives to multiple activities held in rotating, far-flung venues unless someone else pays for them, which raises issues of their independence. That leaves the private sector, not famous for impartiality.

Davos isn't breaking any laws that I know of but it certainly wants to make them. It will probably be soft law at first, which then will have a tendency to harden. I have so far never heard of a TNC that was prepared to work long term for the good of humanity without making a tidy profit at some point in the endeavour. They can all spare good people, even highly placed ones, to participate in GACs and annual meetings because they know it will lead to more business down the road. PPPs are guaranteed to encroach upon public services. They will not be paid for by higher taxes on the private sector, which the largest corporations are notoriously good at avoiding, but by ordinary people as taxpayers or as consumers, or both. We have zero machinery for making these partnerships and corporations accountable to anyone. If the TTIP is adopted, corporate grievances against governments will be arbitrated by private tribunals.

Meanwhile, the elites are strengthening their networks thanks to 'multi-stakeholder governance'. The huge holes in the democratic fabric lead one to ask what will become of accountability, transparency, representation, inclusiveness and management of the commons for the benefit of all citizens.

No one elected the Davos Class, yet its money and power

allow it to confer legitimacy upon whomsoever it chooses and collectively upon itself. Under the leadership of the Global Redesign Initiative, how many foxes will be guarding how many henhouses? And how shall we answer that eternal question – who will guard the guardians?

CONCLUSION

Thank you, reader, for coming this far. I hope you feel suitably, reliably and not too boringly informed about the illegitimate power that has crept into our institutions and our lives via the transnational corporations and their servants. Knowledge is always the first indispensable antidote to feeling, and indeed being, manipulated and powerless. Without knowledge one can do nothing, but it is not enough by itself, only the first step.

This is why I have always tried to be – in the spirit of the Transnational Institute (TNI) which for 40 years has been my intellectual home – a 'scholar-activist'. Sometimes we are called 'public scholars', but the term doesn't convey as well the notion of practising what one preaches. I also think of myself as a 'knowledge worker' and have had the good fortune to do exactly the job I wanted to do.

The scholar-activist tries to use knowledge to help inform and thus build social movements and contribute to campaigns that a sizeable number of people undertake to change situations that cry out to be changed. This can be a long, arduous and sometimes thankless process, both for the knowledge workers and for the campaigners, but things **do** change and I sense that today we may be at a turning point. I have literally never before witnessed so many campaigns on so many subjects in so many countries. What's more, they are increasingly transborder, which is only fitting in the era of the transnational corporation. For years, they, the TNCs, have been far better organized than we have, and now, finally, we're catching up. I'm personally involved in diverse efforts where Europeans routinely get together to plan, strategize and exchange ideas. At TNI, the organizing is often transcontinental.

For the first time, in mid-2014, under the terms of the Lisbon Treaty, the European Parliament was allowed to elect the new President of the European Commission, Jean-Claude Juncker – not exactly direct democracy, but a small democratic shove in the right direction. Juncker's agenda, as set forth in his campaign speech of July 2014, was encouraging.[1] Kindly note: I don't, a priori, share his centre right politics, nor do I expect him necessarily to keep all the pledges he made in his agenda, but in this case that's not the main point. What comes through is that the candidate considered the most conservative of the five running for the office felt that he had to mention many of the activist ideas and goals that were seen as radical 10 or 15 years ago, and has promised to act on them. He calls them his 'political guidelines for the next European Commission' and although the anti-democratic, unresponsive, borderline-devious José-Manuel Barroso administration is never mentioned, much of Juncker's agenda is an unspoken indictment of the past 10 years of European policies.

We know of course that promises are 'only binding on the gullible who believe them', as the French witticism has it, and the French daily experience of living with François Hollande's abject repudiation, one after the other, of his campaign promises doesn't help. Still it seems unlikely that Juncker could renege on *all* his stated aims. He says he wants to make Europe 'the world number one in renewable energies and significantly enhance energy efficiency'. He's for 'stricter controls on banks' and will fight social dumping because 'the same work at the same place should be remunerated in the same manner'. So much for the Bolkestein directive allowing workers to be imported into high-wage European countries to work at their low, home-country wages. Juncker says he wants to 'combat tax evasion and tax fraud' even though we know that Luxembourg is the biggest tax haven in the EU.[2] He even asks for a Eurozone-wide 'financial transactions tax' for which Attac has been campaigning for 15 years.

Juncker continues with his virtuous selling points. If we need to support EU countries in financial difficulty, it should be with a more 'democratically legitimate and more accountable structure' than the 'troika' and with greater 'national and European parliamentary control'. On the TTIP, he swears up and down and more than once that he will not 'sacrifice Europe's safety, health, social and data protection standards or cultural diversity on the altar of free trade', and he comes out unequivocally against private Investor-to-State tribunals: 'Nor will I accept that the jurisdiction of courts in the EU Member States is limited by special regimes for investor disputes.' He says he wants to get rid of the rules such that the 'Commission is legally forced to authorise new [genetically modified] organisms for import and processing even though a clear majority of Member States is against'. In the context of this book, another particularly welcome promise is this:

> I am also committed to enhanced transparency when it comes to contact with stakeholders and lobbyists. Our citizens have the right to know with whom [European officials] meet in the context of the legislative process. I will therefore propose . . . to create a mandatory lobby register covering the [Parliament,

Commission and Council]. The Commission will lead by example in this process.

So should we all just go home and have a glass of champagne? Certainly not! Here I want to tell the reader that it's proof time, in early February 2015 and from now on I can no longer revise my text. I don't know which way the Greek stand-off with the European Central Bank is likely to go. It could end with the victory of the Troika – and the Bundesbank. Greece could leave the euro and this could cause contagion throughout Europe. Or it could end – as I hope – with the recognition of the democratic vote of the Greek people for Syriza and its programme. I don't know which way the TTIP will go either. Neither the EU nor the USA shows signs of changing that agenda and Europe seems prepared to follow the TNC line and give in to US demands.

What I do know is that Europe has been damaged enough by 10 years of Barroso and his gang[3] and most NGOs working on the issues discussed in this book regarded those two Commissions as Public Enemy – if not Number One then at least Two or Three. So Juncker has got to be reminded of his promises and his stated goals at every turn and embarrassed every time he shows his true colours, as he did when he declared after the Greeks elected Syriza that 'there can be no democratic choice against treaties already ratified'. Many of his commissioners have yet to show their own true, probably ugly, colours. Several have close ties to major corporations in the very sectors they are supposed to be overseeing. This too can lead to tragic outcomes for democracy.

We know that the TNCs are not paper tigers and have cruelly sharp teeth and claws. We also know they will fight no-holds-barred against any efforts to introduce a more progressive agenda. Citizens have a clear and present interest in keeping up the pressure on the Commission to deal with all these issues quickly and fairly. One can keep a copy of Juncker's promises handy and rub his nose in them each time he breaks one. By the end of 2014 he had already weakened crucial aspects of the promise to establish a compulsory register for lobbyists.

However, there's a new consolation. A new instrument for activists has appeared on the scene just as we need it most – reminding me of Hölderlin's favourite line: 'There where the peril grows, grows also what shall save us.' For sure, a new search engine alone can't save us, but LobbyFacts allows the data that appears in the EU lobby register to be crunched more meaningfully than before; to be 'sorted, compared, ranked, and analysed' in ways previously impossible; and it reveals, for example, that among the top 10 corporations, several of the biggest spenders, including Exxon, Microsoft, General Electric or Philip Morris, are first and foremost American corporations. So are the top lobby consultancies that hold more than 670 EU Parliament access passes. You can also find out about law firms and trade associations – just don't forget that we need a compulsory register to begin with in order to start unmasking the full truth.[4]

. . .

Perhaps as you read the beginning of this book you were thinking 'this is all true but not especially new'. This may well be so, but I always try to keep in mind that some – often most – readers will find some things they didn't know or hadn't recognized. This book, if it is like most of my work, will be read by people of quite different nationalities.

I've tried, however, to do more than simply describe how lobbyists go about influencing politicians or transforming private interests into national law and increased profits. Particularly when concerned with trade treaties or other aspects of the international sphere, I've sought to identify the ways in which supranational law is invented, introduced and solidified.

Drafted by groups entirely dominated by business interests, these new legal dispositions have the effect of superseding, even replacing, the visible legislative process in such important public policy areas as taxation, consumer or environmental protection, public health and safety, labour standards, intellectual property and much more.

As for the power of the judiciary, transnational corporations think nothing of supplanting established courts staffed by judges who are, after all, public servants, with handsomely paid private sector arbitrators who can decide that sovereign states owe corporations tens of millions if not billions of dollars in compensation. The TNCs may be more gratified still that their arbitrary arbitration rules can cause governments to think twice before proclaiming *any* new law, since almost anything can be construed to have an impact on corporate freedom and thus be challenged by investors.

As things stand presently in our nominally democratic Western countries, all the rules change once you reach the doors of the economy, which isn't even expected to be democratic or ruled by the 'consent of the governed'. The legal instruments that originate in the private sector are created by capitalism itself in a democratic vacuum. Cooperatives aside, business, particularly big business, does not sponsor elections, encourage debate or practise self-correction, save in exceptional circumstances, for example if forced by scandal. Thus it's not surprising that the legal instruments the TNCs invent are even more difficult to comprehend, debate and repeal than are normal, national laws and regulations. TNC law is introduced by stealth; the corporate objective is to replace our habitual legislative, judicial and even executive processes and functions with biased and arbitrary rules that favour maximum profits and capitalist expansion and are for all practical purposes irreversible. No notion of the public good or of citizens' rights intrudes in the gradual replacement of the rule of law by corporate fiat. National sovereignty is overthrown by legal trickery and foolish or complicit governments allow it to happen, perhaps believing that no one is looking.

So I hope I have helped you to look, as well as to understand these frightening new weapons that our democratic institutions will be in a very weak position to counter once they have been put in place.

If they are put in place – and that depends largely on us . . .

Anti-TTIP campaigns in Europe are advancing daily and the scene is changing rapidly. I had finished this conclusion a few weeks ago when a coalition of more than 150 organizations was about to launch a European Citizens' Initiative which – if at least a million signatures in at least seven European member states were collected – would have to be examined by the European Commission. This initiative aimed to have the Commission request that the Council, that is, the member states, withdraw the present negotiating mandate for the TTIP.

This Citizens' Initiative Campaign officially tabled its demand to the Commission in July 2014, leaving the Commission – still the one under Barroso – two months to consider it. In a final burst of anti-democratic fervour, using legal reasoning too arcane to go into here but which lawyers tell us could have been easily refuted, Barroso and Company refused. There will be no official European Citizens' Initiative. The anti-TTIP campaign will nonetheless proceed in collecting the signatures on its own. It will also, simultaneously, ask Juncker to reverse the decision and initiate a lawsuit at the European Court of Justice, but will proceed without waiting for changes, if any, in the legal status.[5]

Underestimating the Barrosian capacity for democratic denial, I had naively written here, 'on the off-chance that [the ECI] is refused – even though it has been double-checked by competent lawyers – then we will campaign against the Commission's obtuse refusal'. That is what we are now doing. We are also going for the same goal, so make sure you sign and that you help meet and exceed your country's quota.[6]

I'm often asked which European institutions will be called on to ratify the TTIP if it comes to that. The future is murky – it could be only the EU Parliament because trade is an exclusive European competence. It could be ratified by national parliaments as well if it was considered a mixed agreement. But beware: the Commission and the Council could agree to allow a provisional entry into force before any ratification at all – even prior to EU Parliament ratification and surely before that of national parliaments. To quote an old European parliamentary hand: 'This provisional application can last as long as the European Parliament or any country has not clearly stated that it rejects its ratification.'[7]

This sounds like a further blow to democracy and so it is – but it should also give hope to the citizens of every European country, even the smallest, because it means that any of the 28 can stop the process right now – or at least once we know for sure what's in the treaty because the negotiators have signed it.

In the United States, there is also a good response to a bad agreement. The anti-TTIP work is led there by the veteran trade campaigners of Public Citizen, founded by Ralph Nader and based in Washington, DC. The Americans have an advantage over Europeans because the Congress can amend trade treaties, not just say Yes or No, as in Europe.

There seems no chance at all that the legislators will give the executive 'fast track authority' this time, which would allow the president to push it through on a Yes/No basis, as has often happened in the past. Members of Congress have witnessed the havoc that previous trade treaties have caused for job creation and want no more of it.

In other words, it's possible to prove that the TTIP is beyond repair and with some hard work, we can force that message on those who run our affairs, no matter how undemocratically inclined they might be. If we want a US–EU treaty – and this need does not seem at all pressing from the NGO side – then it should hew close to another carefully prepared document called the Alternative Trade Mandate (ATM).[8] More than 50 organiza-tions in Europe and dozens more national, regional and network organizations in the developing countries have been part of the ATM's defining and planning process, all of them recognizing that the present, entirely corporate-driven treaty model is fail-ing people, local communities and the environment. In poorer countries, TNCs are assaulting the rights of communities and of the nature that sustains them, giving rise to a number of 'Peoples' Tribunals' to denounce corporate abuses and another international campaign to Stop Corporate Impunity.

The ATM text is a handy summary of what's wrong with the present corporate model: secrecy, negotiations captured by unelected officials, irreversibility, no citizen participation. It signals 10 key issues and, for each, goals to shoot for and processes to undertake to get from where we are to where we ought to be. Utopian? Yes – just like every other reform programme worth fighting for when it was first proposed.[9]

TNC capture of the United Nations and the Davos mission-creep towards seizing authority over every problem known to humankind is tougher simply because we have no democracy beyond our national borders (except for the limited form it takes in the EU). At the international or planetary scale, it's not 'may the best man (or woman) win', but 'the richest stakeholder wins, period'. Rather than going after the Global Compact itself, well ensconced in the UN mother organization, it seems to me preferable to try to team up with organizations of health, food, labour and cultural professionals involved with the UN special-ized agencies who do not take kindly to the presence of TNCs in their high-level policy meetings.

In all these areas and circumstances, we must constantly strike out against the corporate doctrine of self-regulation and the huge fortress that has been constructed around the notion of Corporate Social Responsibility. If a company is already obeying the law and behaving ethically, it shouldn't mind if binding regulations are put in place – it should in fact welcome them as creating a more level playing field.

For the corporate executives who promote and pay for climate denialism, let us reserve special treatment. Something along more medieval lines – say drawing and quartering, iron maidens, heads on lampposts: you get my drift. Anathema is too good for these people. This is not an area where there are two sides to the question. Climate change is happening, humans – particularly those who run the main greenhouse-gas emitting industries – are responsible for it and every year it continues makes it more likely to become irremediable and irreversible, with unpredictable but shattering consequences for everyone. As I write, the Koch brothers in the United States, whose vast fortune is based on oil and gas, are plotting ways to elect their very own denialists to the House of Representatives in the 2014 mid-term elections and change the balance of the Senate to pure Republican. They are preparing to spend half a billion dollars on this effort and the Supreme Court finds this is merely freedom of expression in action.[10]

If the climate criminals were only out to destroy America and America's children, we could say that was the Americans' problem, but they are holding the entire human family to hostage, not to mention every other living thing on earth. I don't know what can be done about them, but at the very least they must be designated as criminals and we need an International Court for crimes against the environment and the human race.

People often ask about boycotts. They can sometimes be useful, but to be successful it's essential that a campaign has a clear goal and chooses a specific company with a well-known brand that has an international presence. They also need contacts with local NGOs in countries where the target is present – otherwise they won't work, at least not in economic terms.

Naming and shaming, however, can always be useful and companies can go over the top hunting down the 'culprits', as the story of Nestlé's spying on Attac shows. Maybe that's one part of a solution for climate crimes and criminals as well.

A mandatory lobby register not just at the EU level but also at the individual country level is an objective to pursue until we actually get them, with teeth. A lot of this work needs to be done by the pros, but those who have other jobs and preoccupations can still send a donation to organizations like the Corporate Europe Observatory, the Transnational Institute, Friends of the Earth and many others. There's a wide choice of formidable, hard-working people spending their days trying to give citizens more control over the companies.

Some quite admirable people still believe that TNCs can be convinced of the error of their ways. I wish them luck but personally think acting on such beliefs is a waste of time. With the resources at their command and the talent they can afford to hire, if the TNCs haven't yet figured out that, say, climate change is real and devastating, that highly unequal societies are undesirable (and bad for business) or that more noble goals than profit and accumulation might exist, then they aren't going to. Everybody else knows such things, for pity's sake!

There's no use denying that the TNCs are the most powerful collective force in the world today, far outdistancing governments that are more often than not in their pockets anyway. I have no magic recipes for changing this situation – just the usual old slogging Gandhian wisdom of 'First they ignore you, then they ridicule you, then they fight you and then you win.' Any activist can provide further appropriate phrases for various other intermediate stages such as 'try to co-opt you', 'lie to you', 'spy on you', etc. And each of the stages can last for an unconscionably long time before you can even cross the boundary into the next one.

Still, I've found that working with others to seek positive

change in the world is the most rewarding way to live. No one can do everything nor everything that needs doing, nor can any of us continue forever. So I'm heartened to be meeting so many wonderful young people who have joined the struggle – so many more than one saw in the 1980s and 1990s when neoliberalism hadn't yet revealed its full capacity to wreak destruction.

We're the minority? Thank God for that! Minorities are where the good new ideas always begin and the seeds of the next struggles are planted and slowly germinate. Minorities put those ideas and issues on the agenda. Majorities finally push things through – as they must do if we are to continue to live democratically. But throughout the long centuries, minorities have always created the spaces where you meet the interesting people, the ones who think, act, hope and love. Personally, I plan to stick with them and hope to meet you there.

ABBREVIATIONS

AGRA	Alliance for a Green Revolution for Africa
AmCham	American Chamber of Commerce
ATM	Alternative Trade Mandate
BITs	Bilateral Investment Treaties
BRICS	Brazil, Russia, India, China, South Africa
CAP	Common Agricultural Policy
CCS	carbon capture and storage
CEO	Corporate Europe Observatory
CETA	Canada–Europe Trade Agreement
COP	Conference of the Parties
CSR	Corporate Social Responsibility
EABC	European–American Business Council
EDF	Electricité de France
EFSA	European Food Safety Authority
ERF	European Risk Forum
ERT	European Roundtable of Industrialists
EU	European Union
FAO	Food and Agriculture Organization

FTAs	Free Trade Agreements
GACs	Global Agenda Councils
GATT	General Agreement on Tariffs and Trade
GDP	Gross Domestic Product
GIs	geographical indications
GMOs	genetically manipulated organisms
GRI	Global Redesign Initiative
HLWG	High Level Working Group
HMOs	Health Maintenance Organizations
IASB	International Accounting Standards Board
IBFAN	International Baby Foods Action Network
ICAP	International Center for Alcohol Policies
ICSID	International Centre for the Settlement of Investment Disputes
ILSI	International Life Sciences Institute
IMF	International Monetary Fund
ISDS	Investor to State Dispute Settlement
MAI	Multilateral Agreement on Investment
MEP	Member of the European Parliament
NGO	nongovernmental organization
NHTSA	National Highway Traffic Safety Administration
PP	precautionary principle
PPPS	Public–Private Partnerships
RCC	regulatory cooperation council
REACH	Registration, Evaluation, Authorization and Restriction of Chemicals
ROW	rest of the world
SIAs	Sustainability Impact Assessments
TABD	Transatlantic Business Dialogue
TEC	Transatlantic Economic Council
TNCs	transnational corporations
TNI	Transnational Institute
TTIP	Transatlantic Trade and Investment Partnership
TTP	Transpacific Trade Partnership

UNCED	United Nations Conference on Environment and Development
UNCITRAL	United Nations Commission on International Trade Law
UNCTAD	United Nations Conference on Trade and Development
UNCTC	United Nations Centre on Transnational Corporations
UNEP	United Nations Environment Programme
UNFCC	United Nations Framework Convention on Climate Change
UNGC	United Nations Global Compact
UNHCR	United Nations High Commission for Refugees
USCC	United States Chamber of Commerce
WBCSD	World Business Council for Sustainable Development
WEF	World Economic Forum
WHA	World Health Assembly
WHO	World Health Organization
WTO	World Trade Organization

NOTES

Introduction

1 Thomas Jefferson, who wrote most of the US Declaration of Independence, included the phrase – astonishing for the time – 'life, liberty and the pursuit of happiness', declaring that it was to 'preserve such values that men instituted government'. The French revolutionary figure Saint-Just is well known for saying 'Happiness is a new idea in Europe'. This strange and original idea was at the core of the struggle for collective as well as individual rights and emancipation.

2 See the 'Six Victories', in Susan George, *How to Win the Class War: The Lugano Report II*, available for download and print on demand at the Transnational Institute, www.tni.org.

3 Paul Krugman, 'Rich Man's Recovery', *New York Times*, 12 September 2013. In fact, 60% of those gains have accrued to the top 0.1% – that is, people with annual incomes of more than $1.9 million. Krugman relies on data from Emmanuel Saez, *Striking it Richer: The Evolution of Top Incomes in the United States* (updated with 2012 preliminary estimates),

University of California, Berkeley, 3 September 2013 (available at: http://eml.berkeley.edu/~saez/saez-UStopincomes-2012.pdf). Income inequality in the United States has been thoroughly explored in earlier publications by Saez and Thomas Piketty.

4 James Surowiecki, 'Moaning Moguls', *New Yorker*, 7 July 2014.

5 I wrote about how they did it in *Hijacking America: How the Religious and Secular Right Changed What Americans Think* (Polity, 2008).

6 Austerity policies have provided a fertile terrain for the rise of far right and sometime fascist movements (Golden Dawn in Greece, for example); the Dutch politician Geert Wilders has specifically called for the expulsion of Moroccans; US prisons have the highest ratio of prisoners per 100,000 of any OECD country, including a huge number of petty drug offenders, usually black or Latino, and so on.

Chapter 1

1 David D. Kirkpatrick, 'Law to Curb Lobbying Sends it Underground', *New York Times*, 18 January 2010.

2 K street is to lobbyists as Wall Street is to bankers. See www.opensecrets.org/lobby/ which gives the statistics on numbers of lobbyists, industry turnover and which industries collectively spend how much.

3 HMOs are businesses, often huge chains. In the *Business Dictionary*, an HMO is defined as a 'US medical firm funded under the Public Health Services Act of 1973. It provides basic and long-term health maintenance and care to voluntary members through a network of doctors, hospitals, and other medical professionals ... enrollees pay a fixed periodic fee for which they are entitled to diagnostic and treatment services including hospitalization, surgery, and prescription medicine, without regard to the cost.'

The OpenSecrets.org blog pages rank separately Top Spenders (companies); Top Industries and Top Sectors. In the latter, 'miscellaneous business', such as the US Chamber of Commerce, is first ($130.7 million), health second ($128.7 million) and finance/insurance/real estate third ($119 million).

4 It's amazing how many Goldman Sachs men – and the occasional woman – turn up in governments and sensitive political positions. George W. Bush's treasury secretary when the crisis erupted in 2007–8 was Henry 'Hank' Paulson, also a top Goldman Sachs man; they have also been found running Italy, Greece and the European Central Bank in the person of Mario Draghi.

5 Roosevelt's final presidential campaign speech announcing the Second New Deal, Madison Square Garden, New York, 31 October 1936. He concluded: 'We know now that government by organized money is just as dangerous as government by organized mob.' Money today, thanks to lobbying, is nothing if not organized.

6 A derivative is a financial product based on some underlying good – sometimes, but not always, a real material good or a financial product based on a tangible asset such as mortgages on real houses. You can check the full range and complexity of available derivatives by going to www.cme-group.com. The CME group is the result of the 2009 merger of the Chicago Board of Trade (founded in 1848, it dealt with foodstuffs and agricultural products) with the Chicago Mercantile Exchange and the New York Metals Exchange; it's the place to look to bet on the evolution of the price of just about anything.

7 See www.bis.org/publ/rpfx13.htm.

8 See the full depressing story in Susan George, *Whose Crisis, Whose Future?* (Polity, 2010), ch. 1, 'The Wall of Finance', and concerning the deregulation of commodities markets, ch. 3, 'The Most Basic Basics'.

9 S. Vitali, J.B. Glattfelder and S. Battiston, 'The Network of Global Corporate Control', *PLoS ONE* 6/10 (2011): e25995. doi:10.1371/journal.pone.0025995 (Public Library of Science).

10 Among the top 50 of the 147 'super-entity', only Walmart and the China Petrochemical Group Company are not financial.

11 Nicholas Copeland, 'Review of the European Transparency Register', *Library Briefing*, Library of the European Parliament, 18 June 2013, p. 2.

12 Dave Keating, 'Campaigners Disappointed by New EU Lobbying Text', *European Voice*, 27 January 2014.

13 This whole story is pretty murky – the German MEP named to head the working group had done nothing for about a year when the Green parliamentary group and *Der Spiegel* revealed that he was a lawyer whose law firm in Brussels was also an unregistered lobbying firm. I'm not taking sides on the basis of much conflicting evidence, except to say that at the very least it shows that lobbying – and keeping it as secret as possible – is a hot topic in Brussels.

14 Tamasin Cave and Andy Rowell, *A Quiet Word: Lobbying, Crony Capitalism and Broken Politics in Britain* (Bodley Head, 2014); Cave and Rowell, 'The Truth About Lobbying: 10 Ways Big Business Controls Government', *Guardian*, 12 March 2014. The authors specifically target the industry in the UK, but their conclusions and generalizations can stand for any other country where lobbyists flourish.

15 See Gary Ruskin, *Spooky Business*, Essential Information, Washington, DC, 20 November 2013. This excellent report summarises what we know so far about corporate spying on non-profit organizations The organization Essential Information was founded by the well-known whistle-blower and social activist Ralph Nader.

16 Many years later, it came out that President Mitterrand had personally approved the operation.

17 Further full disclosure: I am a founding member (1998) of the original ATTAC in France (Association for the Taxation of Financial Transactions to Aid Citizens), served six years as vice-president, am a member of its scientific council and now its honorary president.

18 The judge is now Chief Police Commissioner in his *canton*.

19 José Bové was arrested as a *faucheur volontaire* (volunteer reaper), a movement that began in France in the late 1990s. I testified as a kind of character witness at his first trial, but the only time I ever participated in a *fauchage*, the group of 20-some included a well-known actor, a filmmaker, a French Green parliamentarian and a bishop – with a lot of journalists looking on – unlikely to attract the tender attentions of the police who do their job but understandably don't want to look ridiculous. The real *faucheurs* took real risks and often paid dearly: thanks to them, France has now outlawed GMOs on its national territory.

20 José Bové with Gilles Luneau, *Hold-Up à Bruxelles* (Éditions la Découverte, 2014).

21 Including myself, I hope, since I am leaning on Bové's account for details unavailable to anyone not privy to the inner workings of the EU. Financial corruption is not necessarily involved at such levels; sometimes social status, envy and sympathy with corporate goals may suffice, or favours may be granted to be cashed in later on in one's career.

22 Formerly the Directorate for Health and Consumer Protection. Apparently the final word was judged superfluous.

23 European Medicines Agency (London) and European Chemicals Agency (Helsinki). Both were cited by a European Court of Auditors report in 2012, which stated that there

was 'no effective system in place in these agencies for out-lawing conflicts of interest'.

24 The big four are generally conceded to be KPMG, PriceWaterhouseCooper or PwC, Ernst & Young and Deloitte – all important and powerful TNCs in their own right; all dealing not only with accounting but also with many other consultancy areas, including taxes and how to escape them legally.

25 John Neighbour, 'Transfer Pricing: Keeping It At Arm's Length', *OECD Observer*, January 2002, corrected July 2008.

26 Tax Justice Network, 'Why Tax Havens Cause Poverty', 18 October 2013.

27 See   http://taxjustice.blogspot.co.uk/2013/10/new-report-france-loses-60-80-billion.html.

28 IASB, 'Feedback Statement Agenda Consultation 2011', p. 13, December 2012

29 I suppose it's none of my business how much junk other people eat and drink but I do rather resent that the rest of society has to pay their medical bills (in countries with civilized healthcare systems anyway) or accept the tragic consequences of drunk-driving. See the following section.

30 'Non-Profits Paying a For-Profit Firm', *New York Times*, 17 June 2010. See also the Wikipedia entry on Berman.

31 This section is based on Peter Aldhous, 'The Battle of the Bottle', *New Scientist* 2899, 12 January 2013, and the scientific references the article provides, pp. 42–45a.

32 In the largest class action suit ever tried in the USA, the attorneys-general of all the states came together in 1999 to sue the tobacco companies in order to recover their health-care costs. They were rewarded with a 'Master Settlement' for a 25-year payout of hundreds of billions of dollars from 'Big Tobacco'.

33 The term 'denialist' is deliberately intended to remind

people of Holocaust denialists. The climate Holocaust could be on an unimaginably greater scale.

34 All quotes of Brulle are from Douglas Fischer and The Daily Climate, '"Dark Money" Funds Climate Change Denial Effort', *Scientific American*, 23 December 2013, reporting on Brulle's study, which was published earlier in the scientific journal *Climate Change*. Other information comes from the websites of Donors Trust and Donors Capital Fund.

Chapter 2

1 This chapter is full of (informative) bad news, but opposition to TTIP is growing daily. Hundreds of organizations now oppose it and the media are gradually becoming more attentive to its dangers. Don't allow the grim details to discourage you: this is a battle citizens can win. As of this writing, over a million European citizens have signed a self-organized European citizens initiative to stop the negotiations altogether. Much more will happen before this book is in your hands, but you will still have a chance to be part of the action.

2 Plant as in vegetation, not industry. The WTO agreement concerns 'sanitary and phyto-sanitary measures' (SPS for the initiated), but also human and animal health.

3 David Hartridge, 'What the General Agreement on Trade in Services Can Do': speech at a symposium 'Opening Markets for Banking Worldwide' sponsored by the international law firm Clifford Chance in 1998 and no longer available on their website. I used this quote in my book *Remettre l'OMC à sa place* (Mille et Une Nuits, 2001).

4 It's quite possible the text of Lamy's speech (see next note) reporting this meant to say 4,000 rather than 400. According to UNCTAD, as noted below, by mid-2013 the number of BITs was 3,200 and if one counts all the plurilateral free trade agreements that have an investment chapter,

the figure would be larger. In any case, it's a lot of trade/investment treaties, by nature much harder to follow than the WTO.

5 Director-General of the WTO Pascal Lamy, 'The Multilateral Trading System and Regional Economic Cooperation': speech at the University of International Business and Economics in Beijing, 20 September 2012.

6 At least they're transparent about not being transparent. On 5 July 2013, EU Chief TTIP negotiator Ignacio Garcia Bercero wrote a detailed two-page letter to his US counterpart David Mullaney that the documents regarding TTIP would be marked 'Limited' and 'must be held in confidence', nonetheless 'the documents do not need to be stored in safes'. The EU reserves the right to 'increase the level of protection'. The letter itself is public, so we can't say we weren't warned.

7 As told to, then by, Gérard Choplin, 'USA–EU: L'Europe à l'heure GMT?' Available at: https://gerardchoplin.wordpress.com/2014/02/05/usa-ue-leurope-a-lheure-gmt/. Choplin was formerly European Secretary of Via Campesina, the international small farmers confederation.

8 Total gross world product in 2012 was about $71.7 trillion. The USA has the world's highest GDP: $17 trillion, or 23.7% of the total. The EU is almost equal at $16.6 trillion, or 23% of the total. The partners of the USA in the TTP are worth $11.9 trillion, or 16.6% of world GDP. Taken together, the three groups thus represent roughly 63% of total world GDP. World trade is worth about $18 trillion a year: the US–Pacific share is roughly a third; the US–EU share about 40%, all of which comes to about three-quarters of total trade.

9 European Commission, 'Bilateral Trade Relations, USA, Economic Relations', April 2000 (my italics).

10 For the benefit of readers unfamiliar with French politics,

there is not the faintest lingering trace of 'socialism' in the French 'Socialist' Party or government, as French citizens duly recognized in the 2014 municipal and later European elections. More than 100 of the largest cities in France previously governed by socialist mayors voted in real right-wing administrations. Voters always prefer the original to the copy.

11 Although, as shown in Chapter 1, we don't know which is the biggest-spending lobby, because we have only the pathetic lobbyist's 'voluntary' register, I would bet good money on BusinessEurope. It needn't pay for everything it puts on the agenda either, because it can also place its people on the myriad EU 'expert committees' that prepare a lot of policy decision.

12 See http://europa.eu/geninfo/atoz/en/index_1_en.htm.

13 *EU–US High Level Working Group on Jobs and Growth*, Final Report, 11 February 2013. Available at: http://trade.ec.europa.eu/doclib/docs/2013/february/tradoc_150519.pdf.

14 14 February 2014: 'pour éviter une accumulation de peurs, de menaces, de crispations'.

15 The first or draft mandate was also supposed to be kept secret, but was obtained and published by *Inside U.S. Trade* (www.InsideTrade.com), 29 March 2013, under the original heading 'Strasbourg, 12.3.13 COM(2013)136 final': 'Recommendation for a Council Decision authorising the opening of negotiations on a comprehensive trade and investment partnership, called the Transatlantic Trade and Investment Partnership. between the European Union and the United States of America.' The second or final mandate became available in mid-June 2013 and is marked 'RESTRICTED: Council of the European Union, 17 June 2013. Subject: Directives for the negotiation on the Transatlantic Trade and Investment Partnership between the European Union and the United States of America.'

16 Europe Direct, Letter to the author of 15 November 2013 (Case-ID:0817380/6798447).

17 See www.alternativetrademandate.org.

18 See http://corporateeurope.org/trade/2013/09/european-commission-preparing-eu-us-trade-talks-119-meetings-industry-lobbyists.

19 For details, see CEO, 'Leaked European Commission PR strategy: 'Communicating on TTIP', 25 November 2013, available at: http://corporateeurope.org/trade/2013/11/leaked-european-commission-pr-strategy-communicating-ttip; and George Monbiot's scathing piece, 'Managing Transparency', *Guardian*, 3 December 2013.

20 From the Commission's Q&A on its website which is full of happy and bright misleading information: http://ec.europa.eu/trade/policy/in-focus/ttip/questions-and-answers. The quote is from the report by the London Centre for Economic Policy Research, a highly Establishment think-tank with lots of major banks as 'members', but also the central banks of Europe, including the European Central Bank.

21 Calculated from the Wikipedia figures for the EU economy: GDP for 2013 was nearly €13 trillion ($16.5 trillion).

22 See Roger Bybee and Carolyn Winter, 'Immigration Flood Unleashed by NAFTA's Disastrous Impact on Mexican Economy', available at: http://www.commondreams.org/views06/0425-30.htm; and the Wikipedia entry on 'NAFTA's effect on United States employment', which contains many references.

23 George Monbiot, 'The Lies Behind This Transatlantic Trade Deal', available at: http://www.monbiot.com/2013/12/02/managing-transparency/; also in the *Guardian,* 3 December 2013. Anything Monbiot writes is worth reading and since he writes on many subjects, it's worth keeping up with his website.

24 The Swedish company Vattenfall is suing Germany for €4.4 billion.

25 Various arbitral dispute forums exist: the United Nations Commission on International Trade Law (UNCITRAL) is often used and has drawn up rules governing many others; the International Centre for the Settlement of Investment Disputes (ICSID) is attached to the World Bank; and many others are listed in Wikipedia. The investor and the defending government come to agreement on the venue together.

26 See http://www.nytimes.com/2013/10/19/world/europe/lobbying-bonanza-as-firms-try-to-influence-european-union.html?pagewanted=2&_r=1

27 UNCTAD reports that in 2012, one country, Burundi, made a counterclaim concerning an investor that was suing the government and asked for a modest $1 million. The arbitrators ruled they were competent to decide on the counterclaim, but immediately dismissed it 'on its merits'. That is the only case of a kind of pseudo-reciprocity we know about.

28 Juan Fernández-Armesto, arbitrator from Spain. Originally from the *Global Arbitration Review*, cited by Friends of the Earth Europe in its excellent briefing 'The TTIP of the Anti-Democratic Iceberg', October 2013; available at: http://www.foeeurope.org/sites/default/files/foee_factsheet_isds_oct13.pdf.

29 The best source on all matters concerning ISDS is Cecilia Olivet and Pia Eberhardt, 'Profiting from Injustice: How Law Firms, Arbitrators and Financiers are Fuelling an Investment Arbitration Boom' (Corporate Europe Observatory [CEO] and Transnational Institute [TNI], November 2012; available at: http://www.tni.org/sites/www.tni.org/files/download/profitingfrominjustice.pdf). These two authors have continued their excellent series with further reports; see Olivet, 'A Test for European Stability: The Case of Intra-EU

Bilateral Investment Treaties' (TNI, January 2013; available at: http://www.tni.org/sites/www.tni.org/files/download/briefing_on_intra-eu_bits_0.pdf), and Olivet and Eberhardt, 'Profiting from Crisis: How Corporations and Lawyers are Scavenging Profits from Europe's Crisis Countries' (TNI/CEO, February 2014; available at: http://www.tni.org/sites/www.tni.org/files/download/profiting_from_crisis_1.pdf).

30 Olivet and Eberhardt, 'Profiting from Injustice', p. 8.

31 Hilary Stout, et al., 'Auto Regulators Dismissed Defect Tied to 13 Deaths', New York Times, 8 March 2014.

32 The Rio Declaration on Environment and Development, June 1992, United Nations Conference on Environment and Development (UNCED), sometimes called the Earth Summit. Principle no. 15.

33 Deregulation is the real heart of the TTIP and the corporations are determined to obtain it if not through this treaty, then by some other means. See the next chapter on risk management and 'regulatory cooperation', another fertile field in Brussels.

34 Since the new commission took office in November 2014, the trade commissioner is Sweden's Cecilia Malmström.

35 FAOSTAT gives the 'agricultural population' as 21.7 million in Europe, 5.1 million in the USA. It's not clear exactly who this includes: farm family members, farm workers, servicing activities for farms such as grain storage or tractor repair, etc.

36 See http://www.nppc.org/wp-content/uploads/2013-03-04-Ag-Coalition-US-EU-FTA.pdf. Thanks to Gérard Choplin, formerly responsible for the European branch of the international small farmers' organization Via Campesina for alerting me to the statistics and the US agribusiness letter to their TTIP negotiator.

37 Andreas Geiger, managing partner of Alber&Geiger, a leading EU lobbying law firm, 'American Agriculture,

GMOs and Europe', *The Hill*, Washington DC, 21 October 2013.

38 See the petition addressed to the TTIP negotiators to stop the assault on laws against banning toxic chemicals: http://bit.ly/1eYZhU0.

39 See 'The Agrichemical Lobby Already Laying the Ground Work for the Next Parliament', 7 March 2014; available at: http://corporateeurope.org/agribusiness/2014/03/agrichemical-lobby-already-laying-ground-work-next-parliament.

40 Lone Pine used to be a Canadian company, but changed its name, issued some new stock and incorporated in the US State of Delaware, a US tax haven. It claims it had to invest a lot in getting permits to drill; other reports claim it risks bankruptcy if it doesn't get compensation from Canada.

41 Roger Drouin, 'Contaminated Water Supplies, Health Concerns Accumulate with Fracking Boom in Pennsylvania', *Truthout*, 14 March 2014; available at: http://truth-out.org/news/item/22407-contaminated-water-supplies-health-concerns-accumulate-with-fracking-boom-in-pennsylvania.

42 Dean Baker, 'TTIP: It's not about Trade!', *Social Europe Journal*, 13 February 2014; available at: http://www.social-europe.eu/2014/02/ttip/..

43 The US patent system is notoriously corrupt, or, to be more polite, bizarre. A food company has been able to patent a peanut butter and jelly sandwich because (1) the bread crusts have been cut off and (2) it is in a sealed package. Amazon has a patent on the words 'one-click shopping'. As Dean Baker notes, such frivolous patents are common in the USA and routinely used by large corporations to raise prices and reduce competition.

44 See http://ec.europa.eu/trade/policy/in-focus/ttip/questions-and-answers/. Last updated 12 November 2014.

45 See the CEO, 'Regulation – None of Our Business?', 16 December 2013, and its abundant footnotes for an in-depth

discussion and many proofs of the dangers we are only highlighting here. Available at: http://corporateeurope.org/trade/2013/12/regulation-none-our-business.

46 Cited in CEO, 'Regulation – None of Our Business?'

47 Monique Goyens, quoted in the *Financial Times*: 'Green and Consumer Groups Voice Fears Over EU-US Trade Agreement', 13 October 2013. Goyens adds that the 'very health of European consumers could be put at risk' and 'cites food safety in particular as an issue of concern'.

48 Memorandum, 'Investment Protection Does Not Give Multinationals Unlimited Rights to Challenge Any Legislation', Brussels, 20 December 2013; available at: http://trade.ec.europa.eu/doclib/press/index.cfm?id=1008.

Chapter 3

1 Warm thanks to Ronan O'Brien, who saved me time and trouble by supplying multiple references – not all of which I could use. Regulation involves far more issues and actors than just the TNCs and their organizations, the subject of this book. It deserves a book of its own and Ronan would be the best person to write it.

2 Every time I've quoted this Q&A in public, the audience starts laughing when they hear the 'answers' denying that the TTIP will allow any deregulation at all.

3 For a list of regulatory milestones, see ECORYS, Trade Sustainability Impact Assessment, listing the comprehensive trade and investment agreement between the European Union and the United States of America, Rotterdam, 14 March 2014, pp. 9ff. ECORYS often prepares Sustainability Impact Assessments (SIAs) for the Commission and DG Trade. The ECORYS document cited is the first of a series on TTIP; there should be two more. See also their dedicated TTIP website: http://www.trade-sia.com/ttip/.

4 US Chamber of Commerce and BusinessEurope, 'Regulatory

Cooperation in the EU–US Economic Agreement', October 2012, p. 1 (my italics); available at: http://ec.europa.eu/enterprise/policies/international/cooperating-governments/usa/jobs-growth/files/consultation/regulation/9-business-europe-us-chamber_en.pdf.

5 Carey L. Biron, 'US Plans to Speed Poultry Slaughtering, Cut Inspections', Inter Press Service Report, 9 March 2014; available at: http://www.ipsnews.net/2014/03/u-s-planning-speed-poultry-slaughtering-cut-inspections/.

6 Shawn Donnan, 'US Pushes for Greater Transparency in EU Business Regulations', *Financial Times*, 23 February, 2014. And what great opportunities for American law firms and PR companies in Brussels or in the USA, already poised to pounce when TTIP comes into force.

7 'TTIP: Cross-Cutting Disciplines and Institutional Provisions', *Position Paper – Chapter on Regulatory Coherence*, EU Commission, 2 December 2013; available at: http://corporateeurope.org/sites/default/files/ttip-regulatory-coherence-2-12-2013.pdf.

8 All quotes are from the *Position Paper*. As ever, I am indebted to the CEO – in this case, particularly to Kenneth Haar – whose outstanding work has been often cited herein. See CEO, 'Regulation – None of Our Business?', 16 December 2013, a long and detailed appreciation of the Commission's proposal for a RCC – which might otherwise be labelled 'Unconditional surrender to business interests: Citizens keep out.'

9 In the United States, unless the Congress grants the President 'fast track authority' to sign an agreement and then subject it to a Yes/No vote, Congress has the right to strike down articles or make amendments to the text. In the EU, the European Parliament can only say Yes or No to the package as it arrives from the Commission; no amendments are permitted.

10 Thanks to Kenneth Haar of CEO with his detailed knowledge of EU arcana for pointing this out to me: personal
communication, 27 May 2014.

11 European Risk Forum, Policy Note 25, *The Transatlantic
Trade and Investment Partnership and Regulatory Convergence:
Thoughts from the Risk Forum*, Brussels, December 2013.
Quotes in what follows are from this Policy Note or the
ERF website: www.riskforum.eu.

12 'When a meeting, or part thereof, is held under the
Chatham House Rule, participants are free to use the information received, but neither the identity nor the affiliation
of the speaker(s), nor that of any other participant, may
be revealed.' That includes personal identity, the employer
or the political parties that the speakers or others present
belong to. For more about the Chatham House Rule, see
http://www.chathamhouse.org/about/chatham-house-rule.

13 Warm thanks to Belgian trade union researcher Bruno
Poncelet who brought the Transnational Policy Network
to my attention and gave me the fact sheet he has compiled
concerning it.

Chapter 4

1 I attended the World Food Conference as part of an
Institute for Policies Studies (Washington, DC) team presenting a radically dissenting report against the conventional
wisdom concerning world hunger, omnipresent at the
conference. Disappointed and incensed by the outcome, I
began writing what became my first book, *How the Other
Half Dies: The Real Reasons for World Hunger* (Penguin, 1976).
As I learned more about the agribusiness corporations, I
also made it my business to take on the FAO and attempt
to get rid of its in-house Industry Cooperative Programme,
the source of its sizeable corporate agribusiness presence in
Rome. The FAO eventually buckled under the pressure and

this success is first on my extremely short list of genuine political victories.

2　At a very small dinner in which I was fortunate enough to be included, Boutros-Ghali, an Egyptian, told the story of the US's systematic blackballing of his candidacy, picking off countries one by one through diverse threats or favours called in. Egypt's public debt – particularly for all the armaments it had purchased – was largely held by the United States, and on the morning of the vote, when he saw the Egyptian delegate arrive haggard and white-faced, he knew he was done for. Annan was chosen for his – shall we say – for his positive attitude.

3　*The United Nations Global Compact: Corporate Sustainability in the World Economy*; available at: http://acuns.org/wp-content/uploads/2013/10/GC_brochure_FINAL.pdf.

4　See: http://www.un.org/apps/news/story.asp?NewsID=30429&Cr=global+compact&Cr1=#.VlxrskvlNjE

5　Tom Fawthrop. 'WHO under Siege from Private Sector', Third World Resurgence, No. 257/258, January/February 2012, pp. 2–4. This is a useful article with much detail about private interests in public healthcare.

6　Search 'Agroecology Africa' and note particularly the work of the French Institute for Agronomic Research for Development (CIRAD). The long-term and ongoing work of Jules Pretty (University of Essex, UK) is also especially inspiring.

7　See Susan George, *Whose Crisis, Whose Future?* (Polity, pp. 71ff). Shiva is quoted in David Rieff, 'A Green Revolution for Africa?', *New York Times Magazine*, 10 October 2008.

8　See http://fpif.org/who_under_siege_from_private_sector/.

9　Activists grouped in IBFAN hold that breast-feeding is best for infants, but they are not per se 'against' breast milk substitutes. They simply underline the obvious – that poor mothers in poor countries all too often overdilute the formula, mix it with dirty water and can't feed their babies infant formula under hygienic conditions, so the babies get diarrhoea which can be fatal. Yet poor country hospitals and clinics are often complicit in getting the mothers started on commercial formula feeding. Details of the UN General Assembly meeting can be found at: http://www.un.org/en/ga/president/65/issues/ncdiseases.shtml.

10 IBFAN press release: 'Opening the Door to Business Lobbying – What's Wrong with the New WHO Policy Proposals', 26 March 2014.

11 For a dazzling display of famous corporate logos, go to the World Business Council website, wbcsd.org, and click on 'membership'.

12 Quotes are from the Wikipedia article on the Montreal Protocol. DuPont sensed almost immediately which way the wind was blowing and in the spirit of 'if you can't beat them, join them' made considerable PR capital out of its decision to phase out its CFC production, which is saying something for the world's largest producer. It was from that point on, indeed, a 'good corporate citizen'. See its October 2013 statement at: http://www.dupont.com/corporate-functions/news-and-events/insights/articles/position-statements/articles/montreal-protocol.html.

13 Martin Khor, 'Effects of Globalisation on Sustainable Development after UNCED', Third World Network, 1997 (my italics); available at: http://www.twn.my/title/rio-cn.htm.

14 This quote is included in Kenny Bruno's long report on the first Earth Summit which appeared in the *Multinational Monitor* and gives a wealth of detail on the corporate presence in Rio. See http://www.multinationalmonitor.org/hyper/issues/1992/07/mm0792_07.html.

15 Let me highly recommend a long report by Friends of the Earth, *Reclaim the UN from Corporate Capture*, published in 2012 to coincide with Rio+20. It gives an excellent analy-

sis of corporate progress in infiltrating the UN, as well as case studies, including TNC influence on UN water policy, the Convention on Biological Diversity and the Gates Foundation's penetration of the International Fund for Agricultural Development.

16 See http://corporateeurope.org/environment/rio20. Louise Kantrow's bio on the International Chamber of Commerce is also a kind of capsule history of TNC 'infiltration' of the UN.

17 Also referred to as the Conference of the Parties (COP); the Warsaw conference was COP 19. COP 1 was held in Berlin in 1995; the parties are grouped according to arcane rules, but only the rich ones are expected to pay and to help the poorer ones. This is fair because they started massively emitting CO_2 before the latter, but now that China has become the world's largest economy, as well as its largest greenhouse gas emitter, and other BRICs are catching up, it's also the source of all the internal fights. Many people think that 'COP' is derived from the particularly suspenseful (and well-reported) COP held in COPenhagen in 2008, which turned out to be a dramatic failure. Since then, although climate change has become both more obvious and more severe, media attention has considerably waned and at present the subject, arguably 'only' the most important dilemma that has ever confronted humanity, gets far less coverage. The COP 20 will take place in Paris in late November 2015.

18 In its issue 2959, 8 March 2014, pp. 8–9, the New Scientist published a hopeful-sounding piece by Catherine Brahic entitled 'Lock Up Your Carbon' and, next to it, by Hal Hodson, 'Don't Junk CO_2, Turn It Into Bottles and Glue'. There are concrete plans for Canada's largest coal plant, Boundary Dam in Saskatchewan, to remove and store 90 per cent of its CO_2 emissions beginning in the summer of

2014. It is the 'first big success story' for carbon capture and storage (CCS) but no one knows yet if it can be generalized: is there enough suitable underground storage space? It's more expensive, for now, than other fossil fuel-based energy: will companies pay the extra costs? Can they use less expensive energy to scrub out the gas? Tangible results 'are 10 to 15 years away'. Industry should also start looking at CO_2 as a feedstock instead of as a waste product – this is what 3-M (Scotch Tape, Post-It notes) is doing for its adhesive business. The idea of 'using our own CO_2 to make something we need is very appealing, but I don't know whether the scale will work out', says a 3-M official.

19 CEO, 'Trouble Always Comes in Threes: Big Polluters, the Polish Government and the UN', 19 November 2013; available at: http://corporateeurope.org/climate-and-energy/2013/11/trouble-always-comes-threes-big-polluters-polish-government-and-un.

Chapter 5

1 I heartily second Clinton's judgement: *Global Dreams*, by Richard Barnet and John Cavanagh (Simon & Schuster, 1994) *is* a great book. The late Barnet was co-founder (with Marc Raskin) of the Institute for Policy Studies (IPS) in Washington, DC, and Cavanagh was formerly a fellow and is now director of IPS. In 1974, IPS founded the Transnational Institute of which the present author is board president – IPS and TNI are still sister institutes and still doing their best to tell the truth about the TNCs.

2 See http://www.weforum.org/reports/everybody%E2%80%99s-business-strengthening-international-cooperation-more-interdependent-world. For those who want to take this subject further, I suggest starting simply with the table of contents, accompanied by Harris Gleckman's *Readers Guide*, which gives the bones of it in 15 pages: see

http://cdn.umb.edu/gri_uploads/The_Unique_Design_of_ GRI.pdf. Gleckman, who used to be at the UN Centre on Transnational Corporations (UNCTC) before the Americans forced it to close down in 1994, also wrote an excellent, far more polemical article, 'Multi-Stakeholder Governance Seeks to Dislodge Multilateralism', available at: http://civicus.org/index.php/en/expert-perspectives/2026-multi-stakeholder-governance-seeks-to-dislodge-multilater alism. Another excellent source is David Sogge, a colleague of mine at the TNI. Without David, I would probably not even have known of the GRI's existence. He contributed to TNI's State of Power Annual Report, with a fine piece: 'State of Davos: The Camel's Nose in the Tents of Global Governance', January 2014; available at: http://www.tni. org/sites/www.tni.org/files/download/state_of_davos_chap ter.pdf. My own piece in the same volume is 'State of Corporations', and is an early plan for this book.

3 See   http://www.weforum.org/issues/global-redesign-initia tive.report:2pp.

4 Schwab is probably at least partly responsible for the ubiquitous use of 'governance' as well, which was revived 40-some years ago as 'corporate governance', but is now used for running any sort of institution or country or other collective entity.

5 See http://www.weforum.org/history.

6 Over the past four decades I have witnessed the departure of many excellent people from NGOs, think-tanks or universities into the maw of the likes of the World Bank, the IMF, corporations or other institutions of which, like me, they were once highly critical. I don't blame them – the financial differential is substantial and people often do reach a period in their lives when they seek greener pastures. Needless to say, they disappear, nothing changes in their chosen places of new employment and they are never heard from again.

7 The same or very similar policies are now applied by the Troika – IMF, European Central Bank and European Commission – in Southern Europe, to the same tragic effect: chronic unemployment, especially for young people; dismantling of health, education and social services; mass privatizations; and skewing of incomes towards the wealthiest and increased poverty, etc.

8 However, Nouriel Roubini, who did warn of the crisis, is a member of the GAC on the International Monetary System.

9 See note 2.

Conclusion

1 Jean-Claude Juncker, 'A New Start For Europe: My Agenda For Jobs, Growth, Fairness and Democratic Change. Political Guidelines for the next European Commission': speech delivered to the European Parliament, Strasbourg, 15 July 2014.

2 Except for Britain and its satellites such as Jersey, Guernsey and the flotilla of Caribbean islands.

3 Making an exception for Michel Barnier, the centre right French commissioner in charge of internal markets who did try to better regulate the banks and, heaven knows, was preferable to the dreaded Charlie MacCreevy and Frits Bolkestein who had preceded him.

4 See CEO press release: 'Hard Facts on Europe's Biggest Lobbyists Revealed for the First Time', 30 September 2014. Erik Wesselius of CEO is one of the main architects of the LobbyFacts project, along with Natacha Cingotti of Friends of the Earth Europe and Max Bank of Lobby Control: see www.LobbyFacts.eu.

5 In December 2014, on the day of his 60th birthday, Juncker – or in this case his effigy – was, in front of the Commission's building in Brussels, officially presented with the signatures of 1.1 million EU citizens, including those of seven countries

meeting their quotas as defined by the Commission. This is the self-organized citizens' initiative, and the target of a million-plus was met in just two months. The campaign continues and should be strengthened.

6 See http://www.citizens-initiative.eu/ Signatures must come from at least seven countries, each of which has met its numeric quota. France's quota, for example, is 55,000. This initiative also asks that the European Parliament not ratify the Canada–Europe Trade Agreement (CETA), which contains many of the same features as the TTIP.

7 Personal communication from the political director and assistant to a group of MEPs who know all the European arcana and inner workings.

8 See: www.alternativetrademandate.org.

9 The issues are: food and how it's produced; creating and protecting jobs and labour rights; preserving policy space to realize human rights; money and how it's invested; banks, speculators and the financial industry; raw materials and how they're distributed; climate change and how the burden is shared; protecting public services; public procurement as a tool for social development; intellectual property with human values.

10 The Republicans won a majority in both the House of Representatives and the Senate. Obama will have to govern by veto and executive orders.

INDEX